Timo Lest, East Timor

Administration and Governance

Author
Mark Burton

Copyright Notice

Copyright © 2017 Global Print Digital
All Rights Reserved

Digital Management Copyright Notice. This Title is not in public domain, it is copyrighted to the original author, and being published by **Global Print Digital**. No other means of reproducing this title is accepted, and none of its content is editable, neither right to commercialize it is accepted, except with the consent of the author or authorized distributor. You must purchase this Title from a vendor who's right is given to sell it, other sources of purchase are not accepted, and accountable for an action against. We are happy that you understood, and being guided by these terms as you proceed. Thank you

First Printing: 2017.

ISBN: 978-1-912483-59-4

Publisher: Global Print Digital.
Arlington Row, Bibury, Cirencester GL7 5ND
Gloucester
United Kingdom.
Website: www.homeworkoffer.com
.

Table of Content

Administration and Governance 1
   Preface *1*
   Social Development *7*
      Health 7
      Education 14
      Professional Training and Employment 26
      Welfare Protection and Solidarity 34
      Development and Social Cohesion 44
      Gender Equality and Domestic Violence 45
      Youth and Sports 49
      Environment 52
      Culture and Heritage 59
      Media – Diversity and Independence 65
   Infrastructure Development *68*
      Roads and Bridges 68
      Water and Sanitation 75
      Electricity 81
      Transportation 83
      Telecommunications 87
      Major project procurement 89
   Economic Development *91*
      Agriculture 93
      Livestock and animal farming 96
      Fisheries 96
      Forests and Protected Areas 98
      Petroleum and Minerals 99
      Tourism 105
      Encouraging Employment Creation 111
      Business and investment environment 112
      Decentralisation 122
      Trade 125
      Industry 127
      Cooperatives 129
   Governance Development *131*
      Planning and Strategic Investment 131

Macroeconomic stability 135
Good Governance in the Public Sector 140
Peace and Stability 149
Defence 151
Security 153
Justice 156
Foreign Policy 163

Timo Lest, East Timor

Administration and Governance
Preface

Following exceptional circumstances, the Sixth Constitutional Government was sworn-in on 16 February 2015. It was considered necessary to reform the Fifth Government thoroughly, to improve Government efficiency and effectiveness and to create synergies around the implementation of the *Strategic Development Plan 2011-2030* in order to provide better services to the population.

This structural transformation aimed to give a new generation of leaders the opportunity to govern not just as Ministers but to lead whole of government initiatives. The purpose has been to prepare the younger generation to take the helm of the nation, through a harmonious and gradual transition.

As such, the formation of the Sixth Constitutional Government is a landmark in the political life of Timor-Leste. This transition in leadership is also important for Timorese democracy because it was based on a pragmatic logic of aiming to serve the national interest above any other political and partisan interests, in order to meet the challenges faced by the country.

This Government brings together the will, the experience, the skills and the abilities that will give shape and content to the commitments made before the people and the voters who have legitimated the Fifth Constitutional Government and who now legitimate the Sixth Constitutional Government.

Despite having a short mandate of around two and a half years, the Government is committed to developing the country. The Government is absolutely convinced that it cannot meet the challenge ahead on its own.

First and foremost, this Government considers that dialogue, conciliation and institutional cooperation, both within the governing team and between it and the other State bodies, are vital for achieving the national development goal.

The Government also vows to work closely alongside Civil Society organisations, the Catholic Church and other churches, and Timorese citizens in general. Under this partnership, everyone will be active, participative and accountable, in accordance with democratic values and principles.

It is an absolute priority for this Government to promote national inclusiveness and unity, by investing in and promoting initiatives from civil society organisations and the media, to nurture democracy and to safeguard the national interest.

This process of transformation for our country requires the participation of us all. We all have rights and duties and we all must participate responsibly in the construction of our State and our Nation. This government wants to establish partnerships in which everyone will be able to have a more active participation through what is known as a social audit, where the indicators of government action are thoroughly reviewed so that by working together we may be able to provide better services to our people.

Governing through dialogue, making the most of constructive criticisms and correcting that which does not yield positive results are commitments that can only be successfully implemented if everyone plays a part. Building an inclusive and tolerant society is only possible when everyone is willing to play a responsible role in national development.

Here as well, the organic structure of the Sixth Constitutional Government is based on the philosophy of continuing the work that has already been undertaken by its predecessors and of honouring their legacy.

This continuity will be reflected in the pursuit of programs and policies that have already been started and that are set out in the *Strategic Development Plan* and in the Program of the Fifth Constitutional Government. It will also address the new challenges faced by the country, as a result of the rapid growth of Timor-Leste. New initiatives are now required to ensure that the entire population benefits from the economic and social development of the nation.

An important and strategic part of this process is ensuring better service delivery to the population, including improving the quality of works and the efficient, effective and accountable use of public resources, giving special priority to 1) the reform of public administration, 2) the harmonisation and standardisation of laws and 3) to tax reform.

The political agenda of the Sixth Constitutional Government will be implemented with professionalism, innovation and skill. It will combat the culture of bureaucratisation that has been growing in public organisations and it will make Public Administration more efficient and more effective.

As such, the new executive, which is focussed on improving the delivery of public services and on demonstrating responsibility and accountability, is led by the Prime Minister and by the Coordinating Ministers. Its structure has also been streamlined in order to enable greater coordination of government activities.

The Coordinating Ministers are the Minister of State and the Presidency of the Council of Ministers and three other Ministers with responsibilities for the coordination of three vital sectors for national development – the social sector, the economic sector and the governance sector.

The implementation of our political agenda is therefore based on the structure and vision of the *Strategic Development Plan 2011-2030*, and in particular:

- ✓ Social Development
- ✓ Infrastructure Development
- ✓ Economic Development
- ✓ Governance Development

Using short, medium and long term measures we will, by 2030, transform Timor-Leste from a low income country into a medium-high income country, with a healthy, educated and safe population and a society that is prosperous and self-sufficient in terms of food.

We must be both humble and ambitious; both understanding and demanding. We must work through dialogue so that everyone is involved in building our Nation. By working with a spirit of unity and solidarity, we may achieve fair and sustainable development.

"All for one and one for all" is the motto for the executive of the Sixth Constitutional Government. "We can do better by working together", is the spirit that should move our society so that we may all build our Nation and make both Timor-Leste and ourselves resilient and able to meet the challenges of today and of tomorrow.

Social Development

The Government recognises that the true wealth of any nation is in the strength of its people. Maximising the overall health, education and quality of life of the Timorese people is central to building a fair and progressive society.

Health

Improving health services is vital for improving living standards. Consequently, the Government continues to be committed to its vision of "Healthy Timorese citizens living in a healthy Timor-Leste". This will require guaranteeing access to health services, improving medical attendance, regulating the national health system and strengthening quality infrastructures and skilled human resources in the area of health.

The Government will be introducing new legislation to regulate the delivery of health services by the private sector and non-profit organisations, to promote compliance with ethical principles and rules applicable to the National Health Service. This will be done complementarily and in accordance with the national health policy. We will also establish standard operating procedures in terms of occupational health and safety, as well as other compliance schemes.

Additionally, the Government will strengthen the health system by building the capacity of agencies that provide support to the training and management of health services and to the delivery of quality care, including the provision of essential medication, medical emergency and referral systems, diagnosis systems and blood supply, and the National Health Institute.

Provision of Integrated Community Health Services

The first contact by most Timorese families with the health system tends to be with the primary health care service provided through the Health Centres located in the Municipal capitals, which refer patients to the Community Health Centres of the Administrative Posts and to the Health Clinics responsible for the provision of community health in the sucos.

In addition to strengthening and improving primary health services, the Government vows to create the necessary conditions to enable remote sucos with populations of 1,500-2,000 to be served by Health

Clinics, which will bring those populations a comprehensive package in terms of health promotion and prevention, treatment and rehabilitation.

We will also carry out a broad set of integrated community health services to the villages more than an hour's walk away from the nearest Health Centre or Health Clinic. These villages will benefit from regular assistance by at least one health professional, who will have health kits, means of transportation and incentives. These health professionals will be contractually bound to remain in the villages for at least three years.

In order to enable this, the Government will be implementing quality management models and improving access, namely through a better use of the existing infrastructure. The Government will also intensify the training and capacity building of health professionals, the expansion of specialised services and health specialisations, and the financial sustainability of the national health system.

Additionally, and in accordance with the National Health Sector Strategic Plan 2011-2030, the Government will develop the necessary human resources in the medium and long term, so that there will be at least one doctor, two nurses, two midwives and a laboratory technician in every suco with a population of at least 2,000.

Consequently, over the next years of governance, every Health Clinic will have one doctor, one nurse or one midwife residing at the respective suco, while the Government trains the minimum necessary human resources for providing quality integrated community health services that are accessible to every segment of the society.

We will be implementing the Community Service Models, such as family health programs and house visits, as well as developing protocols for treating and promptly detecting diseases. The Primary Health Care Guide will be fully implemented, so as to continue the work that was started by the previous Government.

Key Public Health Programs

The Government has achieved remarkable progress in reducing the mortality rate of mothers, infants and children under 5, as a result of improvements in pre-natal care, assisted deliveries and quality post-delivery care, as well as emergency obstetrician and family planning services.

In the area of health care, the Government will focus on improving nutrition and maternal, infant and child health, and on reducing morbidity and mortality rates due to infectious diseases, including tuberculosis, HIV-AIDS and malaria.

As such, we will continue improving the access to and quality of the nutrition services at the health facilities and the communities, including the improvement of the quality of malnutrition education, treatment and prevention, and the coverage of child vaccination against polio, tuberculosis, diphtheria and hepatitis. We will continue the programs seeking to raise awareness and educate the populations on transmissible diseases like HIV-AIDS, tuberculosis, malaria and others.

In regard to the fight against HIV-AIDS, we will develop a program under the National Committee for Combating HIV-AIDS, supporting the social inclusion of sufferers, including the completion of an *Uma Mahon* (located in Tibar) for citizens affected with this disease.

We will also give special attention to non-transmissible chronic diseases, victims of accidents and violence, and access to treatment for people with physical disabilities and mental illnesses, by implementing national strategies and strengthening integrated programs on primary health and hospital attendance and reference.

We will also promote access to health facilities for treating mental illnesses and epilepsy, focussing on the training of health professionals in Health Centres and Health Posts for diagnosing and treating epileptic patients. Additionally, we will raise the awareness of the communities so that they have a better understanding of mental health.

The Government will continue to lay the foundations so that National Hospital Guido Valadares may continue to provide specialised and subspecialised services. In time, it should also support the delivery of reference health services throughout the country.

Services in National Hospital Guido Valadares will continue to be expanded through to 2017, so as to reduce the need for medical evacuations abroad. We will continue the planning process to enable the development of oncology, cardiology and haemodialysis services, in order to respond to the epidemiological changes in the country and to the growing financial implications for the State, as well as for patients and their families, of medical evacuations abroad.

Health human resources and infrastructures

We will ensure advances in the development of initiatives seeking to train and manage human resources in the sector, including policies to ensure the recruitment of adequate and qualified human resources, the improvement of working conditions for health professionals, the deployment of personnel at local level, access to post-graduation specialisations and continuous training. We will develop standards and codes of conduct for health professionals, strengthening technical, ethical and deontological aspects.

As such, we will be establishing a Professional Evaluation Technical Committee in order to draft specific criteria for assessing the performance of health professionals and to contribute to the development of the training and education curricula in the sector of health, in coordination with the Ministry of Education.

Lastly, we will give due attention to the basic infrastructure required for access to quality health services. This will include repairing and rehabilitating Hospitals, Health Centres and Health Posts, which will also be fitted with water supplies and basic sanitation. We will continue to manage transportation in the sector properly, that is, ambulances and multipurpose vehicles. We will also enhance the information and communication technologies required for pursuing the goals of the sector.

The goal set in the *Strategic Development Plan* of building a Health Clinic in each of the country's 442 sucos will continue to be a priority for the Government. Presently there are 272 Health Clinics throughout the country.

The Government will be constructing a new Paediatrics building in National Hospital Guido Valadares, especially dedicated to treating and diagnosing child diseases and sick children. This building will become a specialised and subspecialised centre of national reference.

Education

Quality education and professional training have a strategic importance that influences all other development sectors. The fact that more than 50% of the Timorese population is under 19 years old presents a great challenge to the Government, which must respond to the needs and aspirations of the most representative groups in our society – children and young people.

As such, it is necessary to improve our people's opportunities and to enable our children and young people to fulfil their potential. It is also vital for the social and economic development of Timor-Leste, as we can only aspire to development and progress if our population is educated and healthy.

The Government will continue striving to ensure that all children attend school and receive quality education that imparts to them the knowledge and skills that they require in order to lead healthy and productive lives and to contribute in an active manner to the development of our Nation. For this purpose, the Government will strengthen administrative and financial management, proper planning, institutional coordination, human resources and infrastructure, and invest in outcome-oriented goals enabling better service delivery in the education sector.

Similarly, we will be working in order to improve teacher competences and skills, while training new teachers with a strong pedagogic and scientific component. We will also ensure that teachers have the necessary conditions for performing their noble task of imparting knowledge to our children. Nurturing the learning and teaching of Portuguese, as well as promoting its use in the teaching of science, mathematics and other fields of knowledge, will also be priorities over the next two and a half years of the Government.

Pre-school education

Pre-school attendance gives children substantial advantages in their later education, however rates of attendance in Timor-Leste are very low. To ensure that Timorese children get a strong start in their education, the Government will expand and improve pre-school services to provide comprehensive early childhood care and education, especially for our most vulnerable and disadvantaged children.

After having approved the new National Pre-School Education Policy and having drafted and approved the National Pre-School Base

Education Curriculum, we will now ensure their implementation and monitoring, as well as make available teacher training programs and quality teaching and learning materials. It is important that teaching and learning are based on identified needs and on the best practice in terms of child development programs.

Over the next two and a half years the Government will continue building at least 250 new pre-schools and refurbishing all presently degraded classrooms, so that there is a sufficient number of classrooms in every geographic area of the country. All new schools and classrooms will be properly equipped.

The Government will also continue developing broad theoretical and practical training programs for pre-school teachers, who will be trained in pedagogic methodologies that are appropriate to pre-school education. Consequently, the Government will ensure that at least half of all Timorese children from three to five years old receive quality pre-school education and are covered by a new health and child nutrition program that is tailor-made to children of those ages.

Local languages may be used as teaching and learning languages in order to improve access to education and to ensure that children have a sound basis of literacy and numeracy. This will enable a smooth transition for mastering the official languages of Timor-Leste.

The Government will also accredit existing pre-schools and set the minimum criteria for operation, as well as develop the role of Parent and Teacher Associations in the monitoring of teaching and learning. These measures cover both basic and secondary education.

Basic education

Since 1999 Timor-Leste has made great efforts in improving basic education, which currently encompasses the first nine years of schooling. Timor-Leste achieved considerable progress, particularly in relation to training teachers and building schools.

Many challenges remain, however, which include children starting school when they are too old, children dropping out of school, children taking too many years to complete their basic education and girls dropping out of school at a higher rate than boys. Rapid population growth will also create significant future demand for more teachers, classrooms and education spending.

The Government will continue to strengthen the system to provide universal access and will ensure the completion of quality basic education by all children.

Over the next two and a half years the Government will work to ensure:

- ✓ Enrolment of all children in the first year of basic education at the proper age.
- ✓ Reduction of school dropouts, by carrying out the school dropout prevention program in every municipality and achieving the designated targets. It should be noted that the school dropout rate increased from 2.24% in 2012 to 2.3% in 2013 and that currently children still take an average of 11.2 years to complete grade 6.
- ✓ Acquisition of minimum literacy and numeracy skills, based on the recommendations and results of the "multilingual education policy", with checking of ongoing pilot projects.
- ✓ Implementation and monitoring of the new base national curriculum for the 1st and 2nd cycles of Basic Education.
- ✓ Improvement of the quality of the education system, including the continuous training of teachers, and of the new curricular contents, adopting the new methodology centred on the student.
- ✓ Provision of the school buildings and facilities required and proportional to the population growth of school-aged children, continuing to implement the National Community

Rehabilitation Patrimony Program, focussing on the existing infrastructure.

- ✓ Development and implementation of a contextually and pedagogically proper school curriculum, implementing and monitoring the new curriculum for the 1st and 2nd cycles of basic education and providing quality teacher training programs and teaching and learning materials.
- ✓ Continued introduction of new school management mechanisms, enabling the provision of quality education in a manner that is efficient, accessible and sustainable. This approach includes administrative, financial, academic, logistical and human resource aspects, as well as the involvement of teachers, parents and students.
- ✓ Assessment of the current school map, in view of demand and population distribution.
- ✓ Implementation of the National School Transportation Program, ensuring its ongoing operation.
- ✓ Introduction of a new teacher training methodology characterised, in the first instance, by the training of teachers in Portuguese.
- ✓ Development of the annual teacher deployment system.

- ✓ Development of a specific training course for school administration and inspection staff.
- ✓ Expansion of the learning vegetable garden program.
- ✓ Constitution of the Special Fund for School Meals, which is to be integrated with other government programs, including the People's Shop and Cooperatives.
- ✓ Broadcasting during the day of educational programs produced by the Ministry of Education.
- ✓ Promotion of the creation of municipal libraries, which are to be provided with a significant quantity of books.
- ✓ Establishment of a communication network between the 22 central basic schools, using intranet and teleconferences.

Secondary education

The Government will ensure that all students graduating from basic education have access to secondary education. This will involve expanding access to secondary education, providing adequate infrastructure, training qualified teachers in secondary schools and adopting proper curricula to respond to the country's development needs. This will ensure better access to the labour market and greater encouragement to students so as to advance to higher education.

Secondary education in Timor-Leste is divided into general secondary schools and technical secondary schools. General secondary education seeks to prepare students to advance to higher education, while technical secondary education seeks to prepare students to enter the job market and to enable them to have access to technical higher education and to university education.

In order to achieve these educations goals the Government continue to:

- ✓ Considerably increase the capacity of secondary schools to absorb a greater number of students completing basic education, as well as expand the current secondary education system throughout the country.
- ✓ Continue to implement an infrastructure program for building modern schools in accordance with the set standard.
- ✓ Start a program of Technical Centres of Excellence in various municipalities, in the areas of economy, agriculture and engineering, as well as in courses related with the sectors of services, tourism and hospitality.
- ✓ Implement and monitor the new curriculum for general secondary education and for technical and vocational secondary education.

- ✓ Improve the quality of teaching through broad requirements in terms of teacher training and qualification by introducing new methodologies concerning the training of teachers and their continuous training.
- ✓ Develop and implement a school administration and management system guided by the schools themselves.
- ✓ Develop the ESTV – Secondary Technical and Vocational Schools – in order to create professional avenues for secondary students, including by way of partnerships with strategic development sectors (agriculture, fisheries, tourism and energy).
- ✓ Create curricular practice laboratories at secondary schools.
- ✓ Introduce new management mechanisms to ensure that every Secondary School has the required and proper learning manuals and materials.
- ✓ Encourage the teaching of cross-disciplinary competences in terms of entrepreneurship and cooperatives.
- ✓ Carry out external audits to foundations receiving public transfers.
- ✓ Promote the creation of private school associations.

- ✓ Hold national competitions to determine the students with the best school performance (kadi kakutak).
- ✓ Develop active cooperation with the Catholic Church and other churches in order to improve the teaching of Religion, Ethics and Moral.

Recurrent education

Recurrent education is meant for persons above school age who did not have the opportunity to attend school when they were of age. Recurrent education incorporates the national literacy program, post-literacy courses and programs of basic education and equivalence.

The Government worked to eliminate illiteracy by 2015. So far, 6,390 students have completed the post-literacy course. In 2015 the Government will conduct a survey of specific data on Recurrent Education, so as to determine the progress obtained by the national literacy campaign.

The Government also estimates that over 15,000 people will be taking part in the post-literacy program by 2017.

The Government will also continue improving the National Equivalency Program regarding basic education by designing and implementing a quality curriculum. This goal will be continued over the following years.

The Government will continue with the goal of establishing Community Learning Centres, in partnership with the World Bank and UNESCO. Out of the total 16 Community Learning Centres foreseen, 10 are already in operation. The other six will be identified and built.

Part of this project includes the drafting of the legal diploma regulating recurrent education and the equivalences between Recurrent Education and Formal Education Programs, by introducing proper transitional mechanisms between formal education and recurrent education.

Higher education

Stronger higher education is vital to build our human resources and to ensure our national development. The Government will promote an efficient polytechnic and university sector in order to provide the children of our people with the opportunity to receive quality education and to take part in the construction of our country.

In order to achieve this goal throughout the next few years, the Government will:

- ✓ Implement standards and criteria ensuring the quality of higher education, guaranteeing that every national qualification is recorded in the National Qualifications Framework.
- ✓ Continue to develop and support the National Agency for Academic Assessment and Accreditation (ANAAA), which is responsible for determining standards and criteria that guarantee quality higher education.
- ✓ Continue to promote partnerships with higher education agencies.
- ✓ Continue to develop a harmonious and efficient systems for coordinating Government interventions with every Higher Education Agency.
- ✓ Establish three Higher Polytechnic Institutes, as well as a Fishing Academy.
- ✓ Implement a sound quality assurance system, recording all national qualifications in the National Qualifications Framework.
- ✓ Continue improving the quality of education at the UNTL.
- ✓ Build a modern compound for the Faculty of Engineering, in Hera.

- ✓ Develop and support the activities of the National Science and Technology Institute to carry out investigations and research involving applied sciences.
- ✓ Promote the connection between Technical and Vocational Secondary Education and Technical Higher Education.
- ✓ Develop the Institute for Training of Teachers and Education Professionals (INFORDEPE), centred on the continuous training of teachers.
- ✓ Regulate the equivalence regime for academic degrees and other qualifications in terms of national courses.
- ✓ Determine the policy for long-distance education, in partnership with SEFOPE.
- ✓ Develop an online library.
- ✓ Promote the participation by national authorities in academic and school activities at every level.
- ✓ Develop a policy for deploying qualified staff in remote areas, so as to nurture the education system.

Professional Training and Employment

Improving the professional qualifications of the Timorese people is essential for the social and economic development of the Nation and for creating dignified employment.

Timor-Leste faces critical constraints in terms of human resources to work in the private sector and in public services under the administration of the State, including in key sectors such as health and education. For our Nation to be able to develop, it is urgent to respond to the lack of skills, particularly with young people, the unemployed and people living in rural areas.

Developing skills are vital for achieving our goal of facilitating access by all Timorese to the labour market, to higher per capita income and to the possibility of being actively involved in the nation building process. It is also important to give women equal opportunities in terms of education and professional training, as well as to enable them to enter the labour market and to contribute to national development.

During the last few years we have made significant progress in building a modern training system in Timor-Leste. We have a National Qualifications Framework that provides qualifications for accredited training and we are creating training sub-Commissions in every major industry. A Timor-Leste Technical and Professional Education and

Training Plan was endorsed and implemented in 2012, so as to guide and develop this sector. This training system being developed will give our people the skills to take up job opportunities in the petroleum, tourism and hospitality, agriculture, construction, maritime and vehicle industries. New training will also help people residing outside of Dili, and particularly in remote areas, to start new enterprises and businesses.

In order to continue building on these solid foundations, our training system will have to be allocated more resources. This will enable it to train a skilled workforce and to promote access to the job market.

The Government will continue providing the necessary leadership for developing skills in our country and acting in several key areas, including:

- ✓ The national traineeship system, with the support of the new National Council for Skills, Employment and Productivity. This system will place students training in companies, while encouraging those companies to develop a skilled workforce.
- ✓ Supporting a training system that encourages the delivery of quality training by government, industry, community and non-government accredited providers, and

- ✓ Expanding the national qualifications standards to include all major occupations and ensuring national curricula and materials for all registered training programs.

National training commitment

The Government implemented the National Training Commitment, approved by Parliament, which will ensure that, by the end of 2015, 50% of all school graduates who do not enter work or continue with education after completing school will be offered a funded accredited training program.

The program started in 2013 with 2,500 training places to provide a pathway for students requiring training to enter the labour market or to create their own businesses. The Government will ensure that women and men are provided with equal access to this training. The Government will continue this professional training program, so as to ensure an average of 2,500 training places every year.

The National Training Commitment will be a two-pronged one:

- ✓ The National Training Ticket provides fully funded training for one year and is delivered by an accredited training organisation in a classroom or workshop setting. Students have also been placed without pay in a local business, so as to acquire work experience.

✓ The National Traineeship Program provides students with a combination of theoretical learning and on-the-job experience in local industries. This will enable the introduction of on-the-job training in Timorese industry, while enabling trainees to enter the job market. All students graduating successfully from the National Traineeship Program will obtain a national qualification certificate.

National labour content policy

The Government will continue implementing a National Labour Content policy to establish requirements for the employment and training of Timorese people in national projects.

The National Labour Content policy will continue requiring all major businesses to ensure that a minimum percentage of the value of labour in all major projects in Timor-Leste is dedicated to the employment or accredited training of citizens of Timor-Leste. Timor-Leste will continue to welcome international businesses as partners in the development of our Nation and the National Labour Content Policy will continue applying the equitable regulations that have been set in relation to all of our partners.

The policy applies to international businesses operating in Timor-Leste and to all government contracts. This policy is being implemented following consultation with the Timor-Leste Chamber of Commerce and Industry, the National Council for Skills, Employment and Productivity and the Civil Society.

The Government will continue promoting the development of and compliance with the rules concerning work conditions, prevention of occupational risks, placement and protection of employment through the Inspectorate-General of Labour, as a public entity whose main goal is to regularise key aspects in the labour market, in the promotion of worker rights and in the improvement of working conditions.

As such, the Government will seek to strengthen and nurture the resolution of labour conflicts that may arise from individual and collective work relationships through mediation and conciliation mechanisms, in strict compliance with the principles of impartiality, independence, procedural fairness and justice.

Investing in qualified trainers, national training materials and training facilities

The Learning Resource Development Centre is already working to raise professional standards of trainers and provide teaching and learning materials to accredited training providers, including Technical High Schools and Polytechnics.

Meeting our country's training needs over the next 20 years, and implementing the Timor-Leste National Training Commitment, will require training facilities and infrastructure to be used by public and private registered training organisations. We will also continue requiring modern training materials and skilled trainers.

The Government will increase its investment in teaching and learning facilities, as well as in human resources, so as to be able to achieve the goal of providing skilled training. The Government intends to use the 'e-Education' system, which will accelerate youth training. This will include:

- ✓ Development of more skilled and professional trainers.
- ✓ Development of candidates/students who are skilled and prepared for entering the job market abroad.
- ✓ Development of education and professional training infrastructure and facilities.
- ✓ Development of training curricula with relevance to the actual needs of the country, such as in the industrial area.
- ✓ Establishment of a Petroleum and Gas Training Centre.
- ✓ Embedding training as a core activity of businesses.

- ✓ Linking local economic development and local businesses to training services.
- ✓ Establishment of a Public Finance Management Training Centre.

Municipal needs and municipal skill centres

It is important that all Timorese citizens have the opportunity to develop their skills and that all municipalities may provide access to skills and training centres to enable the development of the local economy. The Government will continue reviewing the skills needs of each municipality in terms of economic and social development. This review will guide the establishment of Government and non-Government Municipal Skill Centres, which will provide accredited training.

In addition to providing accredited training, these centres will encourage young people to enter the labour market, provide career guidance and vocational advice, make referrals to training providers, support women entering the labour market, implement employment programs and promote self-employment by developing entrepreneurship and teaching business skills.

International guest worker programs

Timor-Leste has entered into international partnerships to enable Timorese workers to participate in international guest worker programs. South Korea and Australia are currently offering successful programs. These programs provide invaluable international experience and training to young Timorese women and men, as well as providing significant income for the participants and their families.

The Government will continue providing extensive support to these initiatives and work to expand existing programs and to develop new ones. This will include recruiting participants in accordance with the best practices, as well as extensive pre-departure training to ensure that Timorese workers are able to make the most of these international opportunities and then come back to Timor-Leste to support the development of our strategic industries.

Welfare Protection and Solidarity

Ensuring minimum wellbeing standards in society, meeting human basic needs, protecting citizens against social risks, combating poverty and promoting development are the cornerstones of Welfare and imperatives for modern states.

Building on these principles, one of the challenges that is put to Government is how to draft and design a coherent welfare system that is based on the integration and complementarity of a set of public policies, programs and services seeking to promote a more efficient and effective fight against poverty, as well as the improvement of wellbeing in the communities.

And since it is by working with the populations on the ground that one can understand their social problems and make changes, the Government wants to focus more systematically on supporting Welfare Institutions and on creating Social Attendance Services within territorial delegations. Bringing services closer to the population requires the existence of "welfare officers" with specific professional skills, which makes it extremely important to invest in the training of future welfare officers.

Consequently, the Government will continue supporting and protecting our children and young people, families in poverty, the elderly and the citizens who work and who contribute to national wealth. The goal is to ensure lifelong protection, without neglecting special conditional protection for specific groups. This protection will continue to be done through money transfers, in-kind (goods and services) support and indirectly by supporting Social Agencies that serve the populations, within a perspective of integrated work and partnership.

Concerning Veterans, the Government will strive to solve pending problems. In turn, the Government demands seriousness and honesty in registration statements.

Continuing the effort to build the vital institutions of the country, the Government will contribute to the creation of the Welfare State set in our Constitution. This should improve economic efficiency, reduce poverty and promote social equality, social inclusiveness and the autonomy of citizens to achieve their human potential.

Contributory welfare

In order to guarantee the principle of *substitution of income* for people who work and, at a certain time of life, lose that income (due to old age, disability, maternity, etc.), the Government will adopt and expand the current transitional welfare scheme, to create a definitive scheme that is based on a single mandatory and contributory system that guarantees social security to every worker and their dependants, including in the public sector and at least for the situations currently foreseen in the transitional scheme (old age, disability and death/survival).

Social contributions shall be extended to other events in accordance with the priorities and revenues foreseen for social security (mostly through contributions).

The entry into force of the definitive and contributory welfare scheme will not entail the loss of acquired rights of civil servants who currently benefit from the transitional scheme, although they will constitute a "closed group".

Non-contributory welfare schemes

Old age protection - the elderly

Based on the principle of *income redistribution*, the Government will continue to guarantee a basic pillar of welfare to every elderly citizen not covered by the contributory welfare scheme, making sure that they receive the elderly support allowance (SAII). Over the next two and a half years, the Government intends to complete the research on the need to revise this allowance or to introduce new protection measures, as well as to draft a strategic policy for providing specific support to isolated or homeless elderly persons.

The Government will also provide additional in-kind support (mostly food) to vulnerable elderly persons and financial and in-kind support to agencies that house or assist the elderly.

Children and youth protection

Children and young people constitute the large majority of the national population and represent the future of our country. Children and youth protection is a priority for the integrated welfare scheme to be developed by the Government.

Therefore, within a perspective of ensuring the essential minimum in terms of welfare for these age brackets, the Government will continue protecting children and young people who are part of particularly vulnerable families through the Bolsa da Mãe Program – a money instalment that is delivered to eligible families and that can only be used on health and education expenses for the children. Over the next two and a half years the Government vows to improve the program, including coverage and criteria for identifying eligibility.

The Government will also be investing in the drafting of a proper legal framework concerning the Rights and Protection of Minors, including the Child Protection Act, the Adoption Act, the Educational Guardianship Act and a Special Penal Scheme for youngsters aged 16-21.

The Government will also continue protecting vulnerable children, by developing strategies to guarantee that every Timorese child is protected against violence, negligence and abuse. This will give continuity to the programs seeking to educate the communities – families, neighbours, schools, churches and other service providers – on the rights of children and the concept of 'Safe House', particularly in relation to girls and children with disabilities. The Government will also take measures in order to eradicate practices that violate the rights of children, such as early marriage, child labour and other types of exploitation, including domestic violence, sexual abuse, prostitution, human trafficking and negligence.

We will create a free 24/7 telephone line called "child line" for reporting abuses to minors.

The Government will also continue investing in the identification of cases of violation of the rights of children and young people, as well as in the implementation of programs seeking to provide a social response to those situations. Additionally, the Government will continue investing in programs to rehabilitate street children.

The Government will also guarantee the protection of children and young people by way of allowances and in-kind support to private Social Solidarity Agencies that house and support citizens in these age brackets, as well as Day Centres, Homes/Orphanages and "ambulatory" support.

We will also establish a structure for the Commission on the Rights of Children, seeking to promote basic advocacy of children rights, and hold a series of events and workshops protecting and promoting the most elementary rights of children.

Lastly, the Government will be continuing the Program of the National Commission on Child Labour, including the implementation of the National Plan against Child Labour. This will ensure awareness of and effective combat against this form of child exploitation.

Welfare Agencies

The Government acknowledges the vital role played by Welfare Agencies in terms of providing welfare and promoting the wellbeing of the population, particularly in the more isolated regions. As such, over the next few years the Government will be improving and expanding the financial support granted to these agencies, in compliance with set rules. This is unquestionably an important form of welfare that is indirectly guaranteed by the Government, covering various aspects of poverty and human development, as well as citizens from various age brackets (children, young people, adults and elderly persons).

Other Social Support and Services

In order to complement the monetary transfers foreseen under the contributory welfare and non-contributory schemes and the allowances given to private welfare agencies, the Government will also continue providing in-kind support – goods (foodstuffs and others goods) and services (namely funeral cars and welfare coffin services) – to people, households and groups in particular situations of poverty or vulnerability, or who have fallen in special situations requiring emergency responses (e.g. people serving prison sentences, sick people and their families, people evacuated from other municipalities to Dili).

Over the next two and a half years the Government will make it a priority to have national coordination in terms of responding to these situations and providing efficient support.

Since dignified housing is also an important aspect of Human Development, the Government will also maintain the project to provide social housing to vulnerable households – Millennium Houses.

Old age and disability protection – Elderly and disabled people

People considered to be invalid to have a profession are protected by social security in two ways: via the contributory scheme, which grants them a disability pension, in the case of public sector workers or of private sector workers who contributed to the system; or via the non-contributory scheme, which grants a support allowance to disabled persons (SAII), in the case of the citizens who are not covered by the social security (general) scheme. In both cases, the citizens in question must present evidence of their disability. As such, the Government will continue working in an integrated and inter-ministerial manner in order to facilitate this medical certification process.

Additionally, it is known that people with disabilities, even if they are not considered unable to have a job, are often the victims of discrimination or isolation, which makes them particularly vulnerable to poverty and social exclusion. The Government will develop and nurture social and community awareness actions and campaigns on disability and the rights of disabled persons, so as to promote their integration and inclusion. We will also create the National Council for Disabled Persons and study the need and relevance of a new National Policy on Disability, which integrates different areas of Human Development.

In terms of actual and immediate protection, the Government will continue guaranteeing assistance to disabled persons through the services provided at the National Rehabilitation Centre. The Government will also support private agencies housing and supporting these citizens, as well as grant in-kind support (including food and technical assistance).

Veterans

The Government will continue honouring the past and our national heroes. It is important for the dignity of our Nation that veterans receive the respect and support that they deserve. For this purpose, the Government intends to establish Veteran Councils as soon as possible. These councils will work from the Municipalities in order to safeguard the credibility of verification and validation of the records and the completion of claimed and contested proceedings. This will require the participation of former resistance cadres and the non-politicisation of Veteran issues.

The Government will also ensure that Veterans are supported by the permanent welfare scheme. We will also continue honouring their contributions to independence by way of the Timorese Resistance Museum and Archive and the Garden of Heroes in Metinaro. We will continue implementing a system for awarding scholarships to the children of Martyrs and Veterans, giving priority to the more underprivileged families. The Government will continue providing all necessary support for the dignified preservation of our National Liberation History.

Managing Natural Disaster Risks

Managing natural disaster risks continues to be a priority for the Government, as set in the document of the National Disaster Risk Management Policy.

Disaster management is an issue that encompasses several sectors and that has been in the forefront of the agenda of international agencies. Disaster risks concern climate change and the adverse impact of natural disasters, which result in the loss of human lives and property, as well as environmental damage. This puts populations in situations of vulnerability, particularly those living in rural areas.

Solving disaster issues requires public policies that reduce disaster risks and increase the resilience of communities. This entails prevention, mitigation and preparation measures, as well as emergency and recovery responses, which must be integrated within a system of community protection and empowerment.

The risk assessment and mapping within the territory of Timor-Leste, drafted in 2012, identify propensity to events such as floods, tropical hurricanes, draughts and landslides, which expose households and communities to situations of risk and consequent loss of income.

In view of this, the Government has been striving to provide a timely response to affected populations. However, in order to make these responses truly effective, considering the associated emergency and the budget allocated every year, the Government proposes to implement the National Risk Disaster Management Policy, which will guide the public intervention strategy in this area, as well as frame the future Disaster Risk Management Law.

Development and Social Cohesion

The Government plays a central role in the development process and in the fight against poverty. This role, which covers several areas, is assisted by the work of Agencies and the communities. The participation of the communities is very important for protecting the population and for managing, preventing, mediating and solving conflicts. These are requirements for wellbeing and for social peace. However, there are still difficulties within the communities. As such, the Government will continue striving to promote social dialogue and harmony within the communities, by way of actions seeking to train and raise the awareness of the various social agents (including local and community leaders), carrying out activities simulating the resolution of conflicts and enabling communities to be more proactive.

Gender Equality and Domestic Violence

The Government will continue enhancing its commitment to gender equality between men and women in all spheres of life. Gender equality is guaranteed in our Constitution and must be a central consideration of all Government programs and decision making. Women's autonomy depends considerably on the government leading the necessary collaboration between the organs of sovereignty, civil society, religious organisations, NGOs and the community.

We will continue our endeavours to ensure implementation of the Beijing Platform for Action and of CEDAW, so as to guarantee equal rights to women and girls, alleviate women's poverty, address discrimination against women in terms of health and education, and eradicate domestic violence.

Gender equality will become a sector crossing issue because addressing gender equality is a whole of government task that requires collaboration and cohesion between the security, health and education sectors, the Civil Service Commission, the judicial sector and other ministries and agencies. The Government will ensure that gender equality will be encompassed into initiatives, meetings and planning across government administration.

The Gender Integrated Approach has provided gender representation in all government agencies dedicated to national development. However, the Government intends to focus even more on gender in key ministries, such as the Ministry of Agriculture and Fisheries, the Ministry of Health, the Ministry of Social Solidarity, the Ministry of Education, the Secretary of State for Professional Training and Employment and the Ministry of Justice, relying on support from the Secretary of State for Social and Economic Support to Women, which will continue promoting regular meetings between the gender work group at national and municipal level and in each State agency.

The Gender Integrated Approach will continue to be considered when setting national priorities, implementing the *Strategic Development Plan*, drafting annual plans and allocating funds in the General State Budget, as well as when monitoring activities implemented by line ministries.

The Government will promote initiatives seeking to monitor and to ensure a more active participation by women in economic development, including in terms of access to credit, involvement in investment programs and participation within the productive sectors of the country. The Government will also encourage participation by women in political life, including by way of capacity building of women's associations in every municipality and in the Special Administrative Region of Oe-cusse Ambeno, so that they may run for elections in the sucos. Supporting women's associations in order to implement the Action Platform of the Women Municipality Congress will be a key part of this strategy.

Gender based violence is unacceptable in a free and tolerant society and the Government will take strong action to address this problem. With gender based violence being the most common form of violence reported to the police, the implementation of a comprehensive policing agenda including training for police officers on how to protect, prevent and assist will be a Government priority. The Government will increase efforts to provide counselling for victims of domestic violence, expand the capacity for perpetrators to be prosecuted in the justice system and expand health and human services to protect victims.

The Government will expand the number of support centres for victims of gender based violence in the entire country, which will be able to provide the necessary care and support. The Government will also increase training and information sessions for Heads of Suco and Heads of Village, in collaboration with the National Police of Timor-Leste.

The Government will continue promoting public information campaigns in every Municipality, disseminating messages about the Zero Tolerance Policy for violence against girls in the schools and at home. The Government will continue promoting the 'Safe Home' concept, particularly for girls in rural areas.

The Secretary of State for the Social and Economic Support to Women will carry out concrete actions in order to strengthen the implementation of the Domestic Violence Law, including the socialisation of the law and the implementation of the National Action Plan on gender based violence and domestic violence.

Youth and Sports

Timor-Leste's young people are the future leaders of our Nation. They, both boys and girls, will reshape Timor-Leste and contribute to the transformation of our society and economy. We must do all we can to support our youth and provide them with the opportunities they need to gain the experience, skills and values to participate fully in the future of our Nation.

Timor-Leste is a young Nation: over 60 per cent of the population is under 25 years old. Our young people experience high rates of unemployment and many that do have work are engaged in unskilled jobs or precarious employment situations. In today's globally connected world, our young people know that there are many opportunities. However, these opportunities are sometimes not accessible to everyone.

The Government is committed to reversing this situation, not only so that young people will have a different outlook regarding their possibilities, but also to ensure that they have real access to opportunities. This can be achieved by improving the delivery of education and vocational training programs by the Government.

The last survey conducted by the Secretary of State for Youth and Sport in 2014 found that 24% of young people living in rural areas and 15% of young people living in urban areas were unemployed. This highlights a category of marginalized young people that should be addressed as a matter of priority.

As such, the Government will continue giving priority to supporting young people, particularly those in a more vulnerable situation. The goal is to improve their living situation and to promote their access to study and training programs that will enable them to enter the labour market.

This strategy also includes the approval of a National Youth Policy that is updated and adequate to the new circumstances. This Policy will include the National Youth Fund, which will provide direct support to the development of young people.

The Government will also support the development of existing Youth Associations and build new Multipurpose Youth Centres, as well as formalise a coherent and practical structure and legal framework for the National Network of Youth Centres.

Additionally, the Government will be drafting a National Sport Policy and a Strategic Sport Development Plan, which will promote sports as a way of supporting character-building and of nurturing the values of cooperation, fitness and teamwork. The plan will focus on the development of sports as an important part in the lives of people, as they lead to social relations, dialogue, tolerance, ethics and democratic values. The plan will also use sporting activities as the basis for involving young people in education and training activities.

In this sense, and following the approval of the diploma regulating the creation of Sporting Clubs within a simplified regime, the Government will continue promoting and facilitating the creation of sporting clubs in the municipalities, covering several different sports, so as to support the development of a strong national identity and to establish the necessary structure for organising the first amateur football league in the country.

In broader terms, the Government acknowledges the power of sports in terms of uniting people, from activities at village level to national and international sporting events. In addition to supporting local sporting activities, the Government will also encourage and promote physical education and educational sports, which have already been included in the national curricula.

Lastly, the Government will continue promoting sporting facilities and equipment in the municipalities.

Environment

Now that the foundations of a democratic State under the rule of law have been laid, defending social justice for citizens, the Government will continue implementing strategies to meet its Constitutional obligations concerning the protection of the environment and the sustainable management of the environmental resources of Timor-Leste.

The Government will continue to be guided by the 2002 World Conservation and Environmental Development Conference's definition of sustainability: that '*sustainable development is development that meets the needs of the present without compromising the ability of future generations to meet their own needs*'. Sustainable development involves a shared focus on economic development, environmental sustainability and social inclusion obviously supported by good governance.

Our ancestors lived in harmony with the environment using it sustainably to support our families. The Government will draw on the strong bond between the Timorese people and the natural environment to ensure that the economy grows in harmony with the natural environment, which will entail traditional practises like "tarabando" in every suco. The Government aims to make Timor-Leste an international model for sustainable development. This effort will start in our schools, where students will be taught about the importance of the protection and conservation of the environment. This will give students a better understanding of the environment and they, in turn, will pass this understanding on to their children.

The Government intends to strengthen the enforcement of environmental laws and regulations and the promotion of sustainable development in programs of environmental awareness, conservation of environmental resources and other forms of intervention, so as to ensure that national development is achieved in an ecological manner. The goal is to have sustainable economic growth by way of a harmonious interaction between human beings and the environment.

Climate change

The Government acknowledges that Timor-Leste's contribution to the climate change problem is minimal. However, we also understand that we are affected by the pollution created by the economic and industrial powers. This means that we have to continue working cooperatively with the rest of the world to reduce polluting emissions.

Timor-Leste is vulnerable to climate change and our climate may become hotter and drier in the dry season and increasingly variable. Three natural resources – water, soil, and the coastal zone – are susceptible to changes in climate and sea level rises. Coral reefs are also very sensitive to changes in water temperature and chemical composition. These changes could have consequences for agricultural production, food security and our tourism industry, and increase the risk of natural disasters caused by flooding, drought or landslides.

Together with the National University of Timor-Leste, the Government will continue developing the National Climate Change Centre for conducting research and observation on climate change issues, ensuring the collection of data on climate change impacts and encouraging technology innovation to address climate change adaptation and mitigation.

Forests and land and sea conservation zones

The Government will implement the Forestry Management Plan being discussed in Parliament, so as to promote reforestation and sustainable land management practices in Timor-Leste. The Government will also implement the National Policy and Strategy on Bamboo Marketing, which will include the promotion of the cultivation of bamboo for purposes of reforestation and erosion control, thereby complying with the approved legislation concerning the Specialised Investment Agency and the Bamboo Research, Development, Training and Promotion Institute, which seek the economic and social diversification of the country and the harmonious development of natural resources.

Natural conservation zones, or national parks, aim to protect ecosystems by limiting commercial activity; however, research and education, as well as cultural, tourism and recreation activities are permitted. Timor-Leste's first protected area is Nino Konis Santana National Park, which will be a centrepiece of Timor-Leste's tourism strategy. Areas that are sites of international importance for birds have also been identified in Timor-Leste and will be protected.

The Government will also continue promoting other areas within conservation zones, such as Tilomar, Ramelau, Fatumasin, Ataúro Island – Manucoco, Matebian, Kablake, Builo, Clere River, Lore, Paitchao Mountain and Iralalaro Lake, Jaco Island, Diatuto Mountain, Be Male – Atabae, Maubara, MakFahik and Sarim Mountain, Tasitolu, Areia Branca Coast, Curi Mountain and the Irebere and Iliomar Estuaries.

In order to protect and conserve marine biodiversity and our beautiful coral reefs, the Government will continue working with Indonesia and other governments in the region that have signed up to the Coral Triangle Initiative to safeguard the region's marine and coastal biological resources for sustainable growth and the prosperity of current and future generations.

We will continue developing the policy for managing watershed areas and coastal zones, which will include strategies for rehabilitating and protecting mangroves in coastal areas, regulating sand exploitation in various rivers, especially the Comoro River, and for creating buffer zones on river banks and around dams, lakes and coastlines to aid water resource conservation and floodplain control.

The Government will also improve sustainable land management, maintain and rehabilitate forests, and develop sustainable forestry practices by way of means such as:

- ✓ Special forestry legislation backed by improved land tenure arrangements;
- ✓ Reforestation in all degraded areas, especially in sloping areas surrounding Dili;
- ✓ Introducing programs to reduce forest or grass burning practices during the dry season;
- ✓ Replacing firewood use with other energy sources ("fugaun rai-mean" project); and

- ✓ Environmental laws and forestry laws to control activities that cause forest degradation.

Biodiversity

The Government approved the National Biodiversity Strategy and Action Plan, seeking to address the threats against Timor-Leste's biodiversity. The Strategy assesses the threats against both marine and land biodiversity in the country and identifies possible incentives for maintaining that biodiversity. The focus is on preventing biodiversity loss and ensuring that Timor-Leste's biological resources are sustainably managed. This Government will introduce a National Biodiversity Act to regulate the implementation of the action plan. The Government will also give due importance to Nature Preservation, so as to protect and maintain nature in Timor-Leste, namely by way of actions seeking to raise awareness on this issue.

Pollution control

The Government will ensure that we control pollution as Timor-Leste's population and economy grows, so that we don't ruin the pleasure of living in Timor-Leste. We will therefore introduce regulations to control air, water, soil and noise pollution. We will build human resource capacity in the area of environmental quality control, including methodologies used for environmental tests. This will involve establishing an environmental laboratory to conduct tests and carrying out environmental auditing, monitoring, and evaluation of pollution for all activities in every municipality.

The Government will commission environmental studies to find the source of various pollutants. This will include reviewing the activities of hotels, restaurants, workshops, hospitals and markets. Regulations will be introduced so that polluters can be fined for the damage that their actions cause.

Access to more reliable, affordable electricity as a result of the reform of the electricity sector will reduce air pollution from household cooking using wood products. Air pollution in Dili will be addressed by campaigns to reduce forest fires around the city and by introducing laws to regulate emissions from vehicles.

The Government will continue introducing urban waste management guidelines based on environmental regulations to set standards for waste treatment in Dili and other major cities. We will encourage composting, plastic recycling, paper recycling and glass recycling plants. We will continue implementing the urban waste management policy, by providing domestic rubbish bins for waste collection.

The Government will consider a strategy for managing solid waste, covering both the collection and storage of waste and the treatment and reuse of organic waste. Used oils will be collected by tanks, both in Dili and in the municipalities, for reuse, recycling or disposal.

It is extremely important to reduce the amount of plastic bags and bottles clogging up our drains and damaging our marine life. As such, the Government will continue running campaigns to encourage people to use paper bags instead of plastic bags, while developing a recycling scheme for all used plastic materials.

Culture and Heritage

In the past, our culture gave us the strength to endure and to achieve our independence. Now it will help us to secure our future and to strengthen our national identity.

The Government considers that there is a pressing need to valorise the Timorese heritage, the legacy of the past and what we are building today. It is necessary to raise the population's awareness to the need for preserving and transmitting our heritage to the future generations.

Consequently, we will be protecting the cultural heritage – the material and immaterial assets that, due to their value, should be considered as having relevant interest to the cultural identity of our people. For this purpose, we will be encouraging the preservation, modernisation and socialisation of the Timorese culture, as well as supporting the promotion of creative arts within our economic development.

There are a wide range of practices that are part of our creative economy, including weaving, carving, drawing and painting, design, music, acting and all aspects of theatre production, dance, film, radio and television production, writing, publishing and advertising. These practices all involve using creativity and cultural knowledge to generate income and wealth.

Cultural institutions

The Government will continue developing the project of the National Library of Timor-Leste, seeking to provide the country with a cultural reference institution that will support the education system and a national network of libraries, as well as contribute to the improvement of literacy levels within the communities. The project for the design and construction of the future Library is ongoing. The Government has also signed cooperation protocols in order to provide the future institution with the necessary resources – books, magazines, audio-visual records, etc.

The Government will also continue supporting the development of a Museum and Cultural Centre of Timor-Leste in Dili, which will permanently host, display and interpret key Timorese cultural and heritage artefacts. The Centre will hold the geological collection currently on display in the Presidential Palace, the archaeological collection that is now spread throughout several countries and the ethnographic collection, comprising about 1,000 cultural pieces, currently stored in the facilities of the Ministry of Education, in Dili. Additionally, the Museum will provide support to a national network of museums and draft projects alongside the Timorese Resistance Archive and Museum.

The National Library and Museum will be designed and built in accordance with international standards, so that the cultural and sacred objects, paintings, books and other collection items are protected against damage from humidity, fire or other hazards. This will also be necessary to ensure that the many valuable heritage collections being stored in international collections may be returned to Timor-Leste.

The Government will also study the possibility of having the National Library project integrate the National Museum and the Academy of Arts and Creative Cultural Industries, so as to save resources and to provide the city of Dili and the country with a unique and iconic educational and cultural infrastructure that can become an element of national identity, create employment and attract tourists.

Additionally, the Government will establish Cultural Centres in each municipality in order to develop Timorese music, art and dance and to serve as cultural hubs within each region, showcasing not just regional culture but also inter-regional cultural expressions. Each of these cultural centres will have a library, an exhibition space, a small centre for media and new technologies with internet access, meeting rooms and office space. The Government wants to build five Cultural Centres by 2017 and to have at least one centre in each municipality by 2030.

Academy of Arts and Creative Cultural Industries of Timor-Leste

The Government will continue supporting the establishment of the Academy of Arts and Creative Cultural Industries of Timor-Leste. The Academy will begin by training teachers, in order to celebrate traditional Timorese arts such as music, dancing and handicraft. The Academy will also promote creative arts like photography, screen culture and design.

The Academy will include a School of Music for promoting artistic creation in the music sector. The School of Music will operate as a national learning and creative centre, allowing access to music education, the preservation and recording of music traditions, repertoires, songs, dances and instruments, and music research.

The Academy will also include a School of Fine Arts, which will be a centre of research for the visual arts in Timor-Leste and a training venue where artists can develop their technical and artistic skills. The Academy of Arts and Creative Cultural Industries of Timor-Leste will provide education and training in weaving tais, ceramics, jewellery, basketry, wood carving, metalwork, leatherwork and other craft skills and marketing.

The Government will commence plans for a national theatre and dance company, which will be established in the medium term to train actors and dancers and to provide entertainment opportunities.

Cultural heritage

The Government will play an active role in preserving our Cultural Heritage, including traditional houses and historical monuments, immaterial heritage (traditions, knowledge and artistic expressions) and cultural objects. Following the work that has been done, and as the Government is preparing to sign important UNESCO cultural conventions, the area of preserving and promoting the cultural heritage of Timor-Leste should be given special attention, particularly in view of its potential in terms of local development, since it should be able to create jobs, attract tourism and generate wealth.

The Government recognises that it is important to preserve our traditional architectural heritage, particularly Uma Lulik – the sacred houses in which a great part of community life takes place. The Government will approve and implement a Cultural Heritage Act, seeking to protect, preserve and improve the cultural heritage.

Screen culture

The Government recognises the enormous potential of audio-visual technology for increasing people's access to cultural facilities available in Dili and for sharing unique cultural practices across the various municipalities of Timor-Leste. The gradual spread in coverage of television, radio and other audio-visual as a direct result of the electrification program throughout the country will greatly improve access to culture. The government will also be encouraging the growth of a cinema and television sector in Timor-Leste.

Cultural tourism

The Government will continue supporting the expansion of Timor-Leste's cultural tourism sector. Our traditional culture, the living history of our rural communities, our handicraft, our music and our dances will provide visitors with many of their most memorable experiences. The Government will support the development of infrastructure that enables tourism development, including housing, throughout the country's villages, so as to promote cultural tourism. There will also be information for tourists on the internet and religious pilgrimages to locations of significance around Timor-Leste.

Media – Diversity and Independence

The right to information, freedom of expression, and freedom of the press are vital for the consolidation of democracy in Timor-Leste. Circulation of information increases public understanding of government projects and activities and helps build national unity and cohesion. The Timorese people are entitled to objective and impartial explanations of events and projects. Additionally, the Government will be promoting shows seeking to develop ethical, moral and integrity principles – civic education – in the society.

1.10.1 Timor-Leste News Agency

Timor-Leste needs to expand the means for collecting and socialising information on the country throughout the national territory, as well as internationally. The Government will promote studies, prepare the legal framework and train the human resources required for establishing the Timor-Leste News Agency.

National Journalism Training Institute

The Government will support and promote the establishment of a national journalism training institute to improve the capacity of the mass media in the country, including radio, television and newspaper multimedia.

Media Law

The Government will promote the socialisation of the Media Law, which seeks to guarantee, protect and regulate the exercise of the freedom of information, freedom of the press and freedom of the media. The Law will be translated into Tetum and there will be a public information campaign targeting journalists, media bodies, State agencies and the public in general.

Encouraging media diversity

The Government will promote the consolidation of the role of Radio-Television Timor-Leste as a public company, and will provide the required capacity building and materials for the professionalisation of the organisation. In addition, the Government will continue strengthening the capacity of Community Radios as instruments for information and cohesion within the local communities. The Government will also seek to encourage private sector investment in the media in order to nurture a competitive environment and to achieve a diversified, responsible and dynamic media sector.

Press Council

The Government will promote the establishment of the Press Council, which is an independent administrative entity foreseen in the Media Law. This body will ensure that media bodies are independent from political power and economic power, oversee the professional and ethical conduct of journalism professionals and media operators, and ensure compliance with the conditions for becoming and working as a journalist. The Government will provide the necessary support for establishing of the Press Council, including the drafting of the Statute of the Press Council, support to the election of the representatives from journalists and media bodies and the establishment of the entity.

Infrastructure Development

In order to develop our Nation, build a modern and productive economy and create jobs we must build core and productive infrastructure. However, the scale and cost of our infrastructure needs are significant and therefore it is necessary that we plan and implement our infrastructure program in an effective and targeted manner.

This Government makes it a priority to demand professionalism, better planning, cost control and cost-efficiency in this sector. This covers materials, human resources and companies hired by the Government. The existence of quality roads, ports, airports, public buildings, telecommunications and connectivity is vital for the future of Timor-Leste.

Roads and Bridges

Over the next two and a half years the Government will continue the large investment program for upgrading, repairing and improving our extensive system of national, municipal and rural roads, as well as for ensuring that this network is well maintained. The Government will also continue the work started by previous Governments on the maintenance of around 450 bridges in Timor-Leste.

Traffic congestion in Dili continues being a concern. As such, it is necessary to implement a program for improving traffic flow and road safety.

A comprehensive and quality road network is required to support the necessary balance in our national development, facilitate the transport of goods at a reasonable price, allow for the delivery of government services and promote agriculture and the growth of the private sector.

Timor-Leste requires a long term road program beyond this Government's mandate. The Government will therefore implement the vision set out in the *Strategic Development Plan 2011-2030*, in order to:

- ✓ Deliver a comprehensive roads maintenance program;
- ✓ Fully rebuild all national and municipal roads to an international standard by 2020;

- ✓ Construct new bridges to provide all-weather access on major routes within five years and the remainder of national and municipal roads by 2030;
- ✓ Build the road infrastructure required to support the development of the south coast;
- ✓ Establish national standards for a ring road around the country and implement it by 2030.

Rural roads

The Government will focus on rural development, so as to improve access by communities in rural areas to markets and public services. As such, the Government will continue investing in the improvement and maintenance of rural roads, according to the implementation of the Roads for Development Program (R4D). Starting in 2015, the Government will be implementing the recommendations of the Rural Road Master Plan. It is estimated that at least 268 additional kilometres will be rehabilitated from 2015 to 2017.

Until 2017 the Government will be investing in the maintenance of at least 521 kilometres of rural roads already rehabilitated to the minimum standard. Roads connecting municipality centres to administrative post centres will be considered as a priority, since they will support an increasingly greater volume of traffic due to being important links for transporting people and goods. The work will be carried out by local contractors, using labour-based equipment. This will generate a considerable number of jobs at rural and municipal level.

The Government will also carry out a program for building bridges. This program will build and rehabilitate bridges needing to be replaced or repaired.

National and municipal roads

Over the next two and a half years the Government will be starting a major program seeking to improve national and regional roads up to international standards. The Government will continue to consider loans as a source for funding new projects concerning the most vital road connections of the Nation, as a component of the National Road Improvement Program.

The construction works for the Dili – Manatuto – Baucau road connection will start in 2015. The construction of the Baucau – Lospalos (including Lautém – Com) and the Baucau – Viqueque road connections will be started in 2016, once the detailed drawings are completed and after reviewing the progress of the projects funded by way of loans.

The construction of the Maubara – Carimbala, Loes – Mota Ain, and Gleno – Ermera links will also start before the end of 2017. The Manatuto – Natarbora road link will be developed in two stages (packets). The first stage, from Manatuto to the Laclubar crossing, is set for completion by the end of 2017, while the second stage, from the Laclubar crossing to Natarbora, should be completed in early 2018.

This road between Manatuto and Natarbora, which is currently in terrible condition, will be improved to an international standard, so as to ensure a vital road connection between the north and the south of the country. This will promote the development of the south coast.

The other major projects in terms of national roads that are already ongoing and set for completion in 2017 are the Dili – Liquiçá, Tibar – Gleno, and Carimbala – Loes links. These tracts of road also include Tasi Tolu – Tibar, Maubara – Carimbala, and Gleno – Ermera. Roads in the south coast should also be improved up to an international standard. The proposal concerning a motorway from Suai to Beaço has been deferred until all the conditions are met for starting this project.

The Government will also carry out a municipal road rehabilitation program, which will include roads in the Special Administrative Region of Oe-cusse Ambeno, as well as in Ataúro. The targeted projects are considered to be of the highest priority and are based on detailed studies and technical drawings.

Without putting into question the importance of the Tasi Mane Project, which will develop our petroleum industry and boost social and economic development in our south coast, the Government is currently revising the road project from Suai and Beaço, which was scheduled to start between 2012 and 2017. The project is not set to start before the end of the Government's mandate.

Over the next two and a half years the Dili – Aileu – Maubisse – Aituto – Ainaro – Cassa road project will be started. This project will provide another key north south corridor, opening up access to central Timor-Leste and promoting tourism by providing an improved link to the Maubisse and Hatu Builiku tourist zone. Traversing mountainous terrain, the project will require extensive surveying, planning and costing work, the responsibility for which will belong to the Government.

Roads in urban centres and in Dili continue to be considered for improvements. The Government will be establishing a proper improvement, rehabilitation and maintenance program for urban roads. The works on urban roads will be carried out by qualified national contractors, based on public tenders. while design and supervision services will be undertaken by international contractors, in collaboration with national consulting companies.

Until the end of its mandate, the Government intends to carry out a comprehensive (routine and periodical) maintenance program covering all categories of roads, from national roads to rural roads. This is a significant investment program that seeks to maintain infrastructure and thereby prevent their degradation, so as to avoid unnecessary expenses with rehabilitation and reconstruction. By 2017, it is estimated that the Government will be maintaining a total of 1,426 km of national and municipal roads, in addition to at least 521 km of rural roads.

National motorway ring road

The economic and social development of Timor-Leste requires a National Motorway Ring Road. This motorway will have two lanes in each direction and will provide a ring road around the country. This motorway will be progressively built and the first stage will involve the construction of national roads of only one lane in each direction. During the initial stages, room will be left available for the addition of an extra lane and design, planning and costing for the full highway will be commenced by the Government. The National Motorway Ring Road will be completed by 2030.

Water and Sanitation

It is pressing to have a strategy for managing clean water resources, as well as for managing water supply and basic sanitation services. All these elements are vital for the future of the country, since they improve public health, create new jobs, encourage local development and make it easier to maintain and sustain our valuable water resources and other infrastructure.

The two most significant causes of infant and new-born mortality in Timor-Leste – lower respiratory infection and diarrheal disease – are directly related to a lack of water supply, poor sanitation and precarious hygiene. While access to piped water, a protected well or hand pump, tanker or bottled water has increased from 48% of the population in 2001 to over 66% in 2010, the Government recognises that it is necessary to do more in order to ensure that all citizens have access to clean water and improved sanitation.

The Government considers that it is important to assess opportunities in terms of institutional reforms in the sector of water and sanitation and the creation of a regulatory entity. The Government will therefore invest in major water and sanitation works in rural areas, in urban peripheral areas, in municipal centres, in schools, in clinics and hospitals and in Dili. This investment will not be limited to seed capital.

Instead, it will also include the operation and maintenance of these services.

Rural and municipal water and sanitation

From 2015 to 2017, the Government will install at least 125 water systems in order to improve household access to water in rural areas. In relation to infrastructures, the Government will be supporting access to sanitation in rural areas, by building public latrines, promoting the marketing of sanitation products at reasonable prices and supporting vulnerable households.

Much of Timor-Leste's urban water and sanitation infrastructures, including pumping stations, transmission pipes, valves and tanks, were damaged or destroyed in 1999. The Government will progressively restore this infrastructure, providing safe and secure piped water supply to urban households in all municipal centres, as well as solutions including the construction of sewage collection systems, wastewater treatment facilities and final destination of urban solid waste. According to the *Strategic Development Plan*, the focus will be on areas where the situation is critical, namely Baucau, Manatuto, Lospalos and Suai.

This will be achieved until 2017, by way of:

- ✓ Developing a Master Plan for Municipal Centres, namely Baucau, Viqueque, Lospalos and Same, in order to study solutions and to agree on priorities concerning interventions in the sector of water and sanitation.
- ✓ Developing solutions concerning water supply in Suai.
- ✓ Implementing the Water Supply Master Plans in Manatuto and Oe-cusse.
- ✓ Fixing leaks, rehabilitating damaged pipes and making connections legitimate.
- ✓ Finding and consolidating new water sources.
- ✓ Constructing reservoirs and treatment facilities.
- ✓ Connecting households to the piped water supply.
- ✓ Monitoring and controlling wastewater collection systems in public, commercial, industrial, social and residential facilities.
- ✓ Surveying final destination sites for solid waste.
- ✓ Investing in operation and maintenance programs.

Additionally, the Government will have to start surveying the availability of water resources throughout the entire territory of Timor-Leste, as well as to draft the legal framework for the various uses of water. The Government will also provide safe piped water to all public schools by 2020, through the Water for Schools program.

Water and sanitation in Dili

In order to be able to provide water in sufficient quantity to a larger number of urban households in Dili, the Government will capture additional sources of water to increase current supplies and treat that water to drinking water standards. This will be achieved by sourcing and treating water from bores, streams and other sources, maintaining and improving water treatment facilities, extending the distribution pipework to service areas and connecting additional households to the distribution pipework.

The Government will also rehabilitate existing water supply systems by systematically fixing leaks, repairing faulty pipes, valves and meters, training meter readers and establishing a billing system. Households that are not currently connected to the system will be connected, so that all connections are made legal.

The Government will carry out a feasibility study on possible public-private partnerships (PPPs) within the sector of procurement services in Dili, so as to assess the future situation.

The Government will implement the Sanitation and Drainage Master Plan in Dili, in order to reduce health risks and to encourage economic development. These plans seek to achieve staged improvements to sanitation, as well as to rehabilitate existing sewers and to separate sewage from storm water drainage.

The Dili Sanitation and Drainage Master Plan covers the whole of the Dili populated urban area, which is projected to increase to 240,000 in 2025. By 2025 this population is expected to generate approximately 28,800m³/day of wastewater. We need to act now to be able to manage our future growth.

The Government will target areas containing medium to higher population densities, together with commercial, industrial and institutional areas for priority sanitation improvements. The Government's objective is to establish a sewerage collection system that covers most of Dili. For those areas where direct connection to sewers is impractical, provision will made for isolated septic tanks and a reliable service to pump them out periodically.

The Government program will enable sustainable and properly operated and maintained infrastructures for collecting, treating and disposing of sewage in Dili by 2025. Additionally, the Government will consider a strategy for managing solid waste, including the improvement of the current Tibar garbage dump and other solutions concerning the final destination of solid waste.

Improved drainage

Timor-Leste's mountainous terrain and monsoonal climate result in regular flooding and erosion in rural and urban areas. Erosion and flooding are major causes of roads collapsing and being washed away.

Appropriate drainage channels and flood management plans can help to alleviate flooding and erosion. The Government will undertake necessary engineering survey work to be able to provide local communities with local solutions to drainage problems. Maintenance of existing drains will be key part of these solutions.

The Government will implement the Drainage Master Plan to dramatically reduce Dili's significant drainage and flooding problems.

Catchment areas outside Dili are very steep, rising to around 1,100 metres above sea level about 9 kilometres inland. Waterways running through Dili have a total catchment area of some 280 square kilometres, with the largest of them being the Comoro Stream with a catchment of some 220 square kilometres. 90% of the catchment runoff is discharged to the sea via four waterways; Comoro, Maloa, Kuluhun and Santana. There are two retarding basins, one in the

Maloa stream and another in the Becora stream, designed to reduce downstream flows during storm events. However, they are currently fully silted up and therefore are not operational.

The Government will commission the following works as Stage 2 of the Drainage Master Plan, seeking to reduce the frequent flooding caused by heavy storms.

- ✓ Cleaning and grubbing to clean and remove solid materials including solid waste, sediment and vegetation that have accumulated in the drains;
- ✓ Channel re-sloping or re-grading to steepen the grade or remove high or flat areas in the channels;
- ✓ Construction of retardation basins;
- ✓ Construction of a slope intercepting channel;
- ✓ Improvement of the Kuluhun and Maloa streams;
- ✓ Channel re-shaping to increase the cross-sectional area and hence the flow capacity; and
- ✓ Improvements to road drainage and overland flow paths in order to direct runoff into drainage channels.

Electricity

The Government will build upon the recent upgrade and expansion of the electrical grid in Timor-Leste to provide reliable electricity supplies to the entire country. Electricity is a cornerstone for economic growth and our rural electrification will also provide immeasurable social benefits to our people. We will ensure that the entire population has access to reliable electricity 24 hours a day.

Renewable energies and complete rural electrification will form the two pillars of our electricity agenda. As such, the Government intends to continue the program, in an appropriate manner based on a thorough review of costs and benefits. We shall continue the program to set up solar and wind power facilities, particularly in remote areas. These facilities are easy to install and can provide up to 10% of our energy needs. This is still subject to a review that will inform the decision on the destination of the program.

The Government is considering the possibility of postponing the investments considered for the Lariguto and Bobonaro wind farm, in order to connect them to the National Grid. The Solar Centre to be established in Hera seeks to make the most of solar power and thereby reduce dependence from fuel.

Within the next two and a half years the Government will be introducing means for collecting revenue, thereby increasing national income. The Government will also reduce operational costs and ensure better client support in the electricity sector. Additionally, the Government will assess the situation of this sector, so as to consider the best options and to determine the most appropriate status for the EDTL.

Transportation

Maritime transportation

Maritime transportation enables the moving of larger loads and a greater quantity of loads at a lower cost than air or land transportation. Since Timor-Leste has a sea coast and is still dependent on the importing of foreign goods, the development of this sector requires greater attention. The Government will also make the necessary investment in order to improve the ability of our human resources and to develop institutions, legislation and physical infrastructure, so as to improve this sector.

The expansion of the Timor-Leste economy requires increased sea port capacity on both the north and the south coasts. Seaport infrastructure development is vital for enabling Timor-Leste to import critical goods and equipment to bolster our economy and for building major infrastructure and supporting exports, including coffee, petroleum products, fish, meat, fruits and grains.

We cannot continue to be dependent from a single national port in Dili, which is no longer able to efficiently handle increasing cargo volumes. Timor-Leste also has port facilities at Hera, Tibar, Oe-cusse, Kairabela, Ataúro and Com, but they are in a state of disrepair.

Critically, the ports at Oe-cusse and Ataúro provide the only significant means of access to their regions from other parts of Timor-Leste. There are no ports or small ship facilities on the south coast and all agriculture and industry is completely reliant upon costly and unreliable road transport to the north.

The Government will build a new multi-purpose national port at Tibar with a capacity of 1 million tonnes per year and the ability to cater for commercial cargo and passenger needs. The Tibar Port project will involve building an international standard road from Dili to Tibar, constructing a wharf and onshore facilities and dredging. This large infrastructure project will be built in stages as port demand increases and financing and budget allocations are provided.

The Government will also establish a logistics base for the petroleum sector in Suai, with the centrepiece of this development being the construction of a new port. This facility will open up the south coast to investment and growth and provide an international access point to Timor-Leste. In the near future, the Government intends to establish an intersectorial integrated program for developing port infrastructure in the south coast of the country.

The new Suai Port will provide an entry point for the materials and equipment that will be needed to build petroleum industry infrastructure and plants. It will be a multi-purpose seaport and include a container park, warehouse logistics area and fuel storage facilities. The port may also include shipbuilding and repair facilities. Construction of the port will require a breakwater to provide protection from the waves from the Timor Sea.

The Government will embark on a regional ports construction program, which will include building, repairing or substantially expanding facilities. The projects to be carried out will be:

- ✓ The construction of a port, with a pier, for protecting fisheries between Laga and Lautém.
- ✓ The construction of a port in Ataúro for supporting the transportation of goods and passengers, as well as fisheries and tourism.

- ✓ The construction of a small port in Kairabela, at the Administrative Post of Vemasse, so as to provide close access by sea to the centre of the municipality of Baucau.
- ✓ The construction of a port in Manatuto, which will include the construction of a loading pier with refrigeration facilities, so as to enable the exporting of fish and agricultural produce.

Air Transportation

Despite requiring considerable improvement, air transportation in Timor-Leste has already contributed to the development of the country's economy. Air transportation is also vital for developing other sectors, including tourism. The Government intends to continue its ongoing programs, particularly the development of airports and airfields. Additionally, the Government will focus on the legal and operational aspects of the institutional development program, so as to improve the way in which agencies operate and to improve service delivery.

President Nicolau Lobato International Airport

The President Nicolau Lobato International Airport in Dili is in poor condition and requires substantial improvement and development to meet increasing passenger numbers and to allow larger planes and to operate safely.

From 2015 to 2018, the airport will undergo staged development. The first stage, which will start in 2015, is the elevation (extension) of the capacity of the President Nicolau Lobato Airport through extending the runway and the apron parking area. The second stage, which will start in 2017, is the expansion and modernisation of the airport.

A comprehensive program for assessing the feasibility of municipal airports is scheduled to start in 2016.

Land transportation

The social and economic development of Timor-Leste is also dependent on land transportation. The Government will continue developing land transportation, including improving infrastructure and support facilities for public and private transportation. In addition to physical infrastructure, the Government will also give the proper attention to institutional development, including the necessary legal framework and the establishment of an integrated and intersectorial program for improving traffic flow and minimising car accidents. Promoting road safety is a priority for this Government.

Telecommunications

Effective telecommunications bring people together and supports the growth of businesses and the provision of government services. They connect villages to each other and to other towns and cities, and then to the world. Telecommunications are essential to Timor-Leste's future development including the creation of jobs, the growth of business and the delivery of vital services such as health, education and security.

The world is living in a new era in telecommunications technology that is characterised by new wireless devices and dramatically lower access costs. This new era, which is in part driven by emerging economies, will transform the way in which people do business and are connecting with each other and with the world.

The Government is determined to ensure we are a part of this structural change in global, social and economic relations.

The vision of the *Strategic Development Plan for 2011 to 2030* is that we will have a modern telecommunications network that will connect people in Timor-Leste to each other and to the world, and that will allow us to take full advantage of global telecommunications advances.

The telecommunications market has been liberalised with the introduction of competition and new entrants to the market. This is improving services, increasing coverage, expanding internet broadband access and lowering prices. These landmark reforms are dramatically improving access to affordable, reliable and modern telecommunications services.

The next stage of major telecommunications reform will be connecting Timor-Leste to land and underwater fibre-optic, within a national and international network. The reality for Timor-Leste is that continued reliance on satellite connections for the internet will not enable the country to meet the requirements of a modern telecommunications system. In order to benefit from the global telecommunications network we need access to an underwater cable.

Major project procurement

This Government program provides for the delivery of major infrastructure works including ports, airports and road projects. Given the central role that these projects will play in our development it is important that they are delivered with good governance and cost-efficiency.

In order to ensure our major infrastructure projects are implemented as cost effectively and efficiently as possible, the National Procurement Commission has, in the past, engaged the services of an international specialist firm to oversee the procurement process for large and complex projects.

Working with the Procurement Commission, this international firm supported the management of the procurement process with the highest levels of integrity and professionalism. This includes the planning and scheduling processes, the preparation of bidding documentation, contract negotiations and the awarding of contracts, as well as ongoing procurement and monitoring support during project implementation.

After transferring know-how to our human resources and after providing specific training, the procurement responsibilities are presently ensured by training and skilled Timorese specialists.

The Government will also submit a General Procurement Law that will standardise procurement contracts, templates and procedures in relation to every procurement action conducted by the Government, including major projects.

Economic Development

Timor-Leste is a low income country with an emerging private sector, limited economic diversification and a concentration primarily on agricultural production. However, our country has significant economic opportunities and strong potential to become a middle-income Nation.

The Government aims to develop a flourishing market economy with a strong private sector to provide jobs for our people and ensure that all parts of our Nation benefit from the development of Timor-Leste's natural resource wealth. We also recognise that we cannot rely solely on our substantial oil and natural gas reserves, which is why it is urgent that we diversify our economy. As such, the Government will continue focussing on expanding and modernising our agriculture sector, building a thriving tourism sector, encouraging much higher levels of private sector activity and activating industries, including the growth and expansion of small and micro businesses.

While Timor-Leste faces significant challenges in restructuring our economy to achieve this vision, we have many positive strengths and advantages, including the resilience and determination of our people, substantial oil revenues, rich maritime and other natural resources, and our location in the dynamic Southeast Asia region which is driving much of the world's economic growth. We also have an unspoiled natural environment and a unique culture, heritage and history, all of which offer significant potential to develop a high-value tourism and hospitality sector.

However, these strengths and advantages continue to be outweighed by poor infrastructure across the country and industry, financing and trade constraints. To achieve economic development, the Government will tackle these challenges, barriers and constraints.

The Government continues to assume the vision of the *Strategic Development Plan* that by 2030 Timor-Leste will have a modern diversified economy, with high quality infrastructure including roads, power, ports and telecommunications. Subsistence agriculture will have been replaced by commercial, smallholder agriculture. Timor-Leste will have food self-sufficiency and will be producing a range of agricultural products for world markets including staple foods, livestock, fruit and vegetables and other cash crops, as well as forestry and fisheries products.

The petroleum sector, including oil and gas production and downstream industries, will provide an industrial basis to our economy. Tourism, and in particular eco-tourism, will be a major contributor to the national economy, with light industries complementing and diversifying the economy.

To achieve this vision the Government will develop the Timor-Leste economy around three critical industries: agriculture, tourism and petroleum. In these industries, Timor-Leste has significant advantages due to our natural resources, geographic location and economic profile. These three sectors will be underpinned by a package of policy initiatives to support the growth of the private sector, particularly in rural areas. Improving service delivery here and obtaining results are essential for achieving the development goal.

Agriculture

The Government will encourage a strong agricultural sector to reduce poverty, provide food security and promote economic growth and jobs in rural areas and consequently in the entire Nation. In turn, a growing agriculture sector will also promote rural development.

The first stage of our plan will be to achieve food security. This will be followed by promoting food production for the domestic market. The next stage will be promoting and investing in the improvement of the necessary inputs for ensuring diversification and improvement of the quality of the produce for exporting.

This plan will include working to improve farming practices to boost the production of rice and maize in order to increase domestic food security and increase opportunities, so as to improve rural livelihoods and to reduce trade deficits.

We will continue promoting the improvement of coffee and vanilla production. The Government will also secure the procurement of water for agriculture, invest in irrigation and water collection and storage infrastructures, and support aquaculture activities seeking to expand the fisheries sector.

Food security

The Government will improve Timor-Leste's food security by promoting the use of high yield varieties identified by the Ministry of Agriculture and by applying and using new techniques for harvesting and storing cereal and other grain agricultural products, including beans.

We will encourage the increase of the domestic production and harvesting of rice, as well as the productivity per hectare. In order to meet this goal, the Government will continue investing in the rehabilitation and expansion of irrigation systems and in the improvement of the water supply (continuing feasibility studies regarding the construction of dams for agricultural purposes).

Throughout the next two and a half years the Government will conduct training in order to apply proper technologies, so as to guide farmers concerning the best crops and cultivation methods to be adopted, in accordance with the local circumstances.

Under the National Action Plan titled "Timor-Leste without Hunger and Malnutrition", the Government will continue providing subsistence farmers with access to training and technical assistance, as required for improving local productivity and strengthening the resilience of the communities to climate change and population growth.

3.1.2 Strategies for commodities

The Government will increase capital investment in key crops such as coffee and vanilla, candlenut and palm oil. We will target farmers in this sector with specialist financial and marketing advice and will facilitate the ongoing resolution of issues related to land ownership in rural areas.

Livestock and animal farming

Over the next two and a half years the Government will continue the plan for improving the intersectorial program for breeding cattle and other small animals in designated areas, by way of establishing cooperatives for this purpose. The Government will continue the national extension campaigns, so as to promote basic care in terms of animal health. This will include the promotion of the livestock industry.

This is the only way we can make a significant contribution to improving nutrition security in Timor-Leste by increasing access to fresh meat and dairy protein sources. The Government will continue providing free vaccines for cattle and poultry, so as to increase cattle and poultry populations within the next two and a half years.

The Government will start a new pilot program of vaccination, in order to control brucellosis.

Fisheries

The Government will continue promoting the sustainable exploration of marine resources throughout our 735 km of coastal line, seeking to provide medium and long term nutritional and economic benefits to each of the 11 coastal municipalities. We will continue assisting the expansion of the seaweed culture and promoting the culture of shrimp and crab.

The Government will promote programs supporting commercial fishery activities in the maritime area of the Exclusive Economic Zone, for commercial purposes.

The National Strategy for Developing Aquaculture (2011-2030) foresees the development of aquaculture in order to put an end to food and nutritional insecurity in the country in general and in rural areas in particular. For this purpose, the Government will be investing in the establishment of aquaculture of fishes such as tilapia and other species with commercial and nutritional value, so as to ensure the provision of fish to the central areas of the country and particularly to improve school meals in terms of protein.

The Government will be revising the current commercial fishing licences in the territorial waters and in the Special Economic Zone, so as to ensure the sustainable exploitation of the marine resources and to guarantee greater economic returns for the country in the medium and long term.

Forests and Protected Areas

Over the next two and a half years the Government will continue promoting and investing in reforestation, particularly in affected areas and areas alongside watersheds. Trees to be planted will be native to Timor-Leste and will have commercial value, so as to preserve natural biodiversity and the soils and to minimise the impacts of erosion in the mountains.

The Government will continue supporting ongoing programs related with land and marine areas.

The Government will give special attention to the protection of the existing National Parks, as a sine qua non condition for preserving the country's biodiversity and "gene bank". Additionally, the Government will establish a legal framework guaranteeing the protection of forestry resources and their industrial exploitation for commercial purposes.

The Government will continue supporting and developing forest nurseries, focussing on community nurseries. This will enable the populations to have an effective participation in the reforestation programs and in the programs for conserving soils and biodiversity.

Petroleum and Minerals

The petroleum sector will be the key pillar of our future development – it is critical not only to our economic growth and strength, but also to our future progress as a successful and stable Nation. While developing the sector, we must ensure that Timor-Leste's natural resource wealth is used to build our Nation and improve our people's lives.

Currently, Timor-Leste lacks the core infrastructure, support industries and human resources to fully operate and manage our petroleum sector. This results in the loss of great opportunities for our people and Nation.

The Government will work to secure these opportunities and to expand the petroleum industry so that it provides a strong foundation for the structural transformation of the Timor-Leste economy into one based on successful petroleum, industrial, export and service industries with a mature and expanding private sector. The Government will work alongside the relevant Ministries to assess the potential in terms of economic diversification.

The Government will make the most of our oil and gas wealth with the development of our National Petroleum Company, TIMOR GAP, E.P., developing the Tasi Mane project on the south coast. We will ensure the skills and experience that our people need to lead and manage the development of our petroleum industry. We will also continue our unwavering commitment to transparency in accounting for revenue from the petroleum sector.

In order to meet the challenges ahead, the Government will take the following steps:

- ✓ Revenue from petroleum will continue to be fully transparent and used to support social and economic development;
- ✓ The petroleum industry will be developed in a way that operates with the maximum participation of Timorese citizens and businesses;
- ✓ The human resources necessary for the operation of the petroleum industry will be improved and developed; and
- ✓ The south coast will be developed to support the expansion of our domestic petroleum industry, including the establishment of core infrastructure.

The petroleum sector is our greatest source of State Budget revenue. Timor-Leste is fully committed to the earnings from our petroleum resources being fully transparent so that everyone can see the financial returns, the movement of public funds and the return on petroleum fund investments. This commitment will be demonstrated through strict and continued adherence to international transparency mechanisms such as the Extractive Industries Transparency Initiative (EITI).

The Government will also work to ensure that our people benefit not just from the revenue from our petroleum resources, but from the full participation management and employment in the petroleum industry. In this way, we can increase the gains to our people beyond the simple selling of oil and gas.

To enable the full participation of our people in the building of the petroleum industry, we have embarked on an extensive and ongoing program of human resource development. This will include training the Timorese in key areas such as geology, petroleum and chemical engineering, petroleum finance and business and project management. This training is being done through scholarships to internationally recognised higher education institutions, civil service professional development opportunities both within and outside Timor-Leste, the secondment of staff to international oil and gas companies and establishing a training centre for oil and gas operations in a polytechnic to be built in Suai.

Importantly, much of this program, including international and domestic scholarships, is funded through the Human Capital Fund and will ensure that Timor-Leste has the people with the skills and experience to lead and manage the development of our petroleum and mining industry.

Central to the strategy of developing our petroleum industry will be the operation and activity of our National Petroleum Company – TIMOR-GAP, E.P. This company will lead the development of the industry through direct participation, ownership and investment in our petroleum sector. It will provide an avenue for Timor-Leste to have a direct business stake in and benefit from the expansion of the sector. TIMOR-GAP will be committed to building our human resources and domestic petroleum expertise to allow Timorese ownership and participation.

Between 2015 and 2017 the Government will start developing the mining industry, by approving the mining code, transforming the National Petroleum Authority (ANP) into the National Petroleum and Mining Authority (ANPM) and creating our National Mining Company – MINAS DE TIMOR (MdT).

Tasi Mane Project

To allow petroleum development in our country and to provide a direct economic dividend from petroleum industry activities, supporting infrastructure will be developed on the south coast of Timor-Leste. This will be led by the Tasi Mane Project, a multi-year development of three industrial clusters on the south coast which will form the backbone of the Timor-Leste petroleum industry.

The project will involve development of a coastal zone from Suai to Beaço and will ensure that required infrastructure is in place to support a growing domestic petroleum industry. Tasi Mane will include the Suai Supply Base cluster, the Betano Refinery and Petrochemical Industry cluster, and the Beaço Liquefied Natural Gas (LNG)-Plant cluster.

The Government will establish a logistics base for the petroleum sector in Suai. The base will provide capacity for the south coast to develop a domestic petroleum sector along with related and supporting industries and businesses. It will provide an entry point for the materials and equipment that will be needed to build petroleum industry infrastructure and plants. Suai will become a centre for the petroleum industry in Timor-Leste, providing services, logistics, fabrications and human resources. This will include the building of a sea port, a housing complex in Kamanasa, a rehabilitated Suai airport and a heavy metals workshop, as well as ship building and repairing facilities.

The Suai Supply Base will become a national industrial base and logistics platform to drive job creation and economic development on the south coast. It will also support the establishment of petroleum centres at Betano and Beaço.

The Betano Cluster will consist of an industrial park where refinery and petrochemical industries will be located, along with a petroleum industry administration city. The city will provide housing and social services, and form a new base of employment on the south coast.

The establishment of a refinery and petrochemical centre will be achieved through cooperation between the public and private sectors. TIMOR-GAP will play a crucial role in this development. The initial phase will establish a refinery which will produce fuel for domestic use such as diesel, gasoline, jet-fuel and asphalts. In addition, many products from the refinery will be exported to increase our trade in oil and gas products.

The Beaço LNG-Plant cluster will be the area in which the natural gas pipeline reaches Timor-Leste land and where the LNG plant to process the gas will be located. Between 2015 and 2017 the Government will continue conducting the technical studies and clearing the land in order to achieve this goal.

A road will be built between Suai and Beaço in order to connect the three clusters and to support the growth of the petroleum industry. This road will be constructed in stages. Each stage will be developed according to economic need, the growth of the industry and the non-petroleum development of the south coast. The first stage will start in 2015 and should be completed in 2018.

Tourism

Timor-Leste's natural beauty, culture and history can make the tourism industry a unique industry sector and an important avenue for our economic development. A successful tourism sector will create jobs, preserve and promote our history and our culture, and create businesses that both visitors and nationals can enjoy, including restaurants, hotels, leisure and entertainment centres and medium sized industries. Because this sector is in the early stage of its development, the Government will position Timor-Leste strategically as a regional leader in the eco, marine, historical and adventure tourism markets.

The Government will continue facilitating the growth of the tourism industry by rehabilitating infrastructure, including the Dili airport, telecommunications and roads in some of the main tourist routes.

The Government will continue working to build a tourism and hospitality training centre in Dili within the next few years. Tourism Information Centres will also be established in Dili, Lospalos, Balibo and Baucau.

Over the next two and a half years we will expand our tourism promotion marketing activities internationally, including an annual calendar highlighting our special events and our attractions. This will include the provision of small packaged tours that will be promoted in tourism centres in Australia and Indonesia, as well as in the Asia-Pacific region.

The Government will continue promoting and expanding the "Dili, City of Peace" tourism and publicity campaign, which includes the "City of Peace" Marathon, the "Tour de Timor" mountain bike race through each of the 13 municipalities of the country, the Ataúro fishing competition, the annual Darwin-to-Dili yacht rally, the International Dive Photo Contest, the Dili Adventure Race and the Com Fishing Festival. The Government will also continue promoting the National Caravan Festival, which will represent the various municipalities and communities, as well as their main tourist attraction sites. These events will bring tourists to Timor-Leste and will raise the country's international profile. As such, the Government will continue expanding these important events.

The Government will prepare its participation at the Milan World Expo 2015, under the theme "Feeding the Planet, Energy for Life", as another way of raising the country's profile. In 2015 the Government will also be organising the celebrations of the 500th anniversary of the arrival of the Portuguese in Timor-Leste, which will be held in Lifau.

The Government will also work on the "Tourism Master Plan", which foresees a set of actions (physical projects, recovery of infrastructure and execution of works) so as to implement the three special tourist zones below.

Eastern tourist zone

The Eastern Tourist Zone will extend from Tutuala through to Com and Baucau and along the coastal road to Hera. This zone is integral to our tourist offerings and includes pristine tropical beaches, mountain scenery and offers adventure activities and showcases Portuguese architecture and local culture. The government will ensure that Tutuala and Jaco Island continue to be a pristine and authentic eco-tourism experience for our visitors.

We will grow the town of Com into a tourist base for the area and will be linked to the Great North Coast Road. The Government will support the establishment of a premium eco-tourist resort on the seaside in Baucau. The city of Baucau will serve as a base for trekking and cultural tours and the spectacular nearby Mount Matebien. The rehabilitation and widening of the Great North Coast Road will facilitate tourist access to these areas. We will also implement the community tourism project in the area of Vemasse/Caravela.

We will put road markers near the Japanese war tunnels on the road south of Baucau and will highlight areas of national pride in eastern municipalities during the resistance, including Mundo Perdido.

We will continue to promote the Nino Konis Santana National Park as a tourist destination in addition to its status as a nature reserve by establishing a visitors' centre, by the training of local guides and establishing walking tours of this naturally beautiful and historically and culturally significant area of Timor-Leste.

The Tourist Information Centre in Lospalos will provide advice and assistance to travellers in the region and organise homestay accommodation options for visitors as well. The Nino Konis Santana National Park in addition to other areas showcase artefacts and areas which highlight local animist faith, particularly the "Lulik" (Sacred) which arise in our landscape, rocks, animals, streams and objects and deceased ancestors. The rock engravings in Ili Kerekere will also be a tourist attraction, along with traditional dances. The government will promote ways for this part of our heritage to be understood by our people and our visitors.

Central tourist zone

The Central Tourist Zone includes the capital Dili as well as Atauro Island and the beautiful Maubisse region. The Government will undertake a proactive tourist development program in the capital because it serves as the primary gateway into the Nation. We will open the Timor-Leste Tourist Information Centre in Dili to provide information on places of local and national interest as well as provide tourist information at the airport.

We will put markers and information near areas of importance to our national resistance, including the Santa Cruz Cemetery, the National Resistance Museum and Archive, the Commission for Reception, Truth and Reconciliation and the Dare Memorial Centre.

Dili serves as the gateway to the island of Atauro where the government will promote the expansion of the eco-tourism which has begun developing there and will highlight the diving and marine tourism opportunities there.

South of Dili, the town of Maubisse will serve as the base for tourism in this area, including promoting a roadmap from Maubisse to Timor-Leste's highest mountain, Mount Ramalau. Seeking to support this goal, the Government has already rehabilitated the iconic Maubisse Pousada.

Western tourist zone

The Western Tourist Zone includes the Great North Coast Road to Balibo, Maliana, Bobonaro and the Ermera coffee lands. The Great North Coast Road provides access to the beautiful beaches and inland views along this part of our Nation. The Government will continue promoting the Dutch fort in Maubara, the Portuguese fort at Balibo and the Ai Pelo Prison – ruins and future museum. The Government supported the rehabilitation of the fort at Balibo, including building a hotel within the walls of the fort, build a café, and will establish a small museum and place markers to commemorate the history of that place.

The Government will also promote eco-tourism, highlighting areas of coffee cultivation in Ermera and developing community tourism projects in Lois. The Government will also strongly promote the hot springs of Marobo, including improved signage and updating the ruins and the guesthouse in order for the springs to become a highlight of a visit to the Western Tourist Zone.

Encouraging Employment Creation

In order to build our Nation and provide jobs and income for our people, Timor-Leste needs to attract investors, partner with international firms to build infrastructure and support local business throughout the country to start-up and grow.

Potential investors must have confidence that they are in a fair business environment and have certainty about laws, regulations and processes that impact their investment. At the same time, we have to make sure that we retain control of our resources and assets, and set directions for their development that benefit all our people.

The Government will work to ensure that Timorese business people have the skills and support they need to identify business opportunities, start up a business, expand into new areas or markets, or start exporting. There are many areas in which Timorese business people can flourish and create jobs, including in the tourism, agriculture, petroleum and cultural industries. The development of local businesses and our private sector will underpin and drive our national development and the Government will focus on ensuring that our people are provided the support, access finance and business training that they need to succeed.

The Government will continue economic policies for promoting private investment, including reforms to business regulation, access to micro finance, promotion of a National Development Bank and the establishment of Special Economic Zones.

Business and investment environment

The future of our economy requires building a mature private sector. The Government will continue giving priority to the creation of a business and investment environment that supports the development of a diversified private sector and the establishment of new businesses and industries that are essential for creating jobs and for enabling us to make the transition to a non-oil economy.

The Government will continue improving our business environment by addressing key challenges the still dissuade investors. These measures will include improving the ability to:

- ✓ Obtain funding;
- ✓ Enforce contracts;

- ✓ Register businesses, including the simplification of the registration and the improvement of interministerial coordination;
- ✓ Secure land titles and register properties; and
- ✓ Resolve business disputes.

The reforms we have made so far give Timor-Leste one of the most attractive taxation systems in the world for doing business.

As part of the Tax Reform we will be conducting, the Government will review every tax and fee applicable to local companies, so as to ensure that they remain competitive and that they are easy to administrate and to comply with.

We will also continue supporting the strengthening of the Chamber of Commerce and Industry of Timor-Leste, so that it may provide our businesspeople with training, counselling, advocacy and representation.

Additionally, the Government will continue supporting and developing the 'one-stop counter – SERVE', i.e. the Business Registration and Verification Service, as well as the Specialized Investment Agency. Furthermore, the Government will develop "e-Government", so as to ensure an efficient alternative for interacting with the Government.

The current dispute resolution system will be strengthened by improving the capacity of the justice system to resolve commercial disputes and to establish effective alternative mechanisms for solving disputes, including the possibility of using international courts.

Lastly, the Government will also focus on Integrated Sub-regional Economic Development. For this purpose, the Government has created an ad hoc mission for implementing this integrated development platform between Timor-Leste, eastern Indonesia and northern Australia.

Public-Private Partnerships

Building our Nation and diversifying our economy will require cooperation between the public and the private sectors. Public-Private Partnerships can be effective mechanisms for funding and developing major infrastructure projects required for economic diversification. The Government will build on the existing Decree-Law and continue developing processes for the identification, evaluation, and construction of infrastructure through Public-Private Partnerships. This work will continue including the creation of internal capacity to negotiate, supervise and manage Public-Private Partnerships.

Timor-Leste National Development Bank

The development of the Timorese private sector is constrained by limited or no access to credit and long-term finance at affordable rates. Our businesses need credit to invest, expand, purchase goods and equipment and upgrade facilities. There is a significant unmet demand in Timor-Leste for credit so that hotels can be upgraded, retailers can purchase a greater range of stock, houses and offices can be built and construction companies can purchase heavy equipment.

The Government continues committed to establishing the Timor-Leste National Development Bank in order to improve the private sector's access to long term funding. This Bank will enable Timorese companies to grow, create jobs and build the economic infrastructures of our Nation.

The tasks for describing and structuring the National Development Bank are ongoing and feature the support of international partners. This bank needs to be managed in a way that supports market competitiveness in the financial sector and that nurtures the growth of private banking, instead of inhibiting it.

The Government has been supporting the establishment of an institute directed to national investment, so as to assist the companies that contribute to the growth of our economy through clear and rigorous investment directives, independent administrative and commercial operations and higher good governance standards. This institute will contribute to the development of investment opportunities by conducting important strategic and commercial projects.

Timor-Leste National Commerce Bank

Access to credit is a problem for small business people and individuals in Timor-Leste, including those living in our regional and rural areas. Lack of credit prevents the expansion of small businesses, limits the ability of our people to start businesses and inhibits the growth of our economy.

The Government transformed the Microfinance Institute of Timor-Leste into the Timor-Leste National Commerce Bank, which already has branches in every municipality and which reaches the Administrative Posts by way of mobile banking vehicles. The Timor-Leste National Commerce Bank is still expanding its services. The Government will continue supporting the Bank and its expansion, so that it can provide banking and credit services to the entire population, as well as provide access to financial services to Timorese citizens and to micro, small and medium companies, both in urban and rural areas. This will contribute to national development, which naturally includes rural development.

Additionally, the Timor-Leste National Commerce Bank and the ANZ Bank are currently conducting a program to develop Mobile Phone Banking.

Special Economic Zones

In accordance with the *Strategic Development Plan 2011-2030*, the previous Government set the guidelines for the program seeking to develop special economic zones within the national territory.

The Special Administrative Region of Oe-cusse Ambeno and the Special Economic Zone of Social Market Economy of Oe-cusse Ambeno and Ataúro were recently created by Law. This Law establishes an economic and social development policy guided by the principle of social market economy for the territorial areas of Oe-cusse and Ataúro, the latter as a complementary hub of development Special Zone. The principle is inclusive, economically participative and socially diversified. It is also sustained and sustainable, with investments receiving special benefits. The development of infrastructure is considered essential and development is considered a priority.

As such, the Government will continue supporting this project as a new model of economic and social development that can attract foreign and internal investment. The Government has also created a Special Development Fund and established its general purposes.

The benefits from Special Economic Zones include:

- ✓ Promoting industry and service sector development, particularly in targeted sectors;
- ✓ Creating jobs and generating national income;
- ✓ Growing export industries;
- ✓ Creating international business opportunities;
- ✓ Improving national infrastructure.

In the case of Timor-Leste, the implementation of the pilot project of the Special Zone of Social Market Economy will be a pioneer project of integrated development that links social development to economic development. We believe that it will be a success story, in which public investment results in sustainable economic growth.

Additional support for job creation in rural areas

Rural development is a priority concern for the Government as around 70 per cent of our population live in rural areas. Should the current national population growth rate be maintained, the population will grow exponentially within the next few years. The Government will implement policies to guarantee the existence of jobs for young people in rural areas and in the increasingly large urban areas. The

Government will also strive to ensure food security, create jobs and alleviate poverty.

The Government's program for rural development is supported by our overarching plan to develop the Timor-Leste economy around three critical industries: agriculture, tourism and petroleum. It is also supported by a number of specific policy initiatives that aim to drive the growth of the private sector in rural areas.

Widespread and sustainable rural development will not be possible without reliable and ongoing support from other sectors, especially transport and roads, water and sanitation, power, health and education. The rate of progress in rural development will be directly linked to the rate at which the Nation's infrastructure can be rehabilitated and upgraded. In terms of overall rural development in Timor-Leste, the private sector has the potential to play a critically important role in helping to eradicate extreme poverty. This is why the Government will continue supporting the initiatives that provide a viable economic basis for rural development to take place. This will include encouraging diversification into new economic activities as well as improving the efficiency of current activities.

A National Planning Framework

The Government will draft a National Planning Framework for Timor-Leste to guide the acceleration of sustainable economic growth and equitable development from national level to suco level, while protecting Timor-Leste's natural environment. The Government will use the National Planning Framework process to ensure that our agriculture sector is developed in a way that minimises damage to the environment, as healthy rivers and catchments, forests and soils are necessary for healthy, productive farms.

Agriculture production zones and conservation zones will be determined according to factors such as land suitability (soils, slope, altitude and aspect), climate (rainfall and temperatures), current land use, the financial viability of production options, supporting policies and the availability of organic or inorganic fertilisers and pesticides. Agricultural production zones will be recommendations rather than being prescriptive or compulsory. Farmers will be able to decide for themselves what they want to plant, but they will be given access to the best information available about crop and seed varieties most likely to succeed in particular areas.

The National Planning Framework will identify opportunities for development based upon the specific characteristics of certain regions, to reduce gaps in progress between regions and between urban and rural areas and to encourage private sector investment in particular areas. Urban-rural and regional imbalances are inevitable in a fast-changing economy. Good land use and conservation planning will be necessary to address these imbalances and ensure more equitable economic growth and a broader distribution of prosperity across Timor-Leste.

Business Development Centres

Business Development Centres have been established in Baucau, Dili, Maliana, Maubisse, Suai, Lospalos, Ermera, Viqueque and Oe-cusse by the Institute for Business Support (IADE). These centres provide training in how to identify and start a business, improve a business and expand a business.

The Government will extend IADE Business Development Centres to all municipalities and the range of services offered will be expanded to include agribusiness services and others identified through a municipality needs assessments. Partnerships with professional training centres will be sought to provide relevant technical skills training.

We will also continue providing training to staff and trainers – training of trainers – from IADE and Business Development Centres, in order to improve their skills and to ensure that the trainees receive better training. Business Development Centres will continue carrying out tenders and initiatives seeking to promote innovative businesses, which may result in 'Business Incubators'.

Decentralisation

The Government's decentralisation policies will also assist the development of the private sector in rural areas. The Government supports local democratic participation by all citizens and will establish more effective, efficient and equitable public service delivery to support the Nation's social and economic development. The Government will make sure that governance is as close to the people as is possible, so as to enable self-determination, dignity and the realisation of our people's dreams and aspirations.

The Government will introduce a new tier of local government, making each municipal administrative circumscription correspond to a local government unit. The Government will also work with the bodies from the Special Administrative Region of Oe-cusse Ambeno in order to strengthen the administrative decentralisation process and to install local government representative bodies and services, according to the specific context and needs of the region.

Local government bodies and services will receive the necessary means for pursuing their respective missions and for delivering efficient and quality public services to the citizens. For this purpose, we will be developing the administrative and management capabilities of our local administration, so as to introduce systems, processes and procedures of local public management and governance. The Government will continue striving to capacity build and valorise the potential of our human resources, so as to ensure that they can perform the financial and treasury tasks effectively, as well as develop, plan and monitor the execution or management of public programs and the delivery of qualified public services at local level.

By 2017, the Government will develop and carry out the Administrative Decentralisation and Local Government Policy. This will include the reorganisation of Local Administration and the decentralisation in the latter of a set of decision-making competences enabling it to provide local public services and, following a positive performance evaluation, decentralises competences by returning them to the local government and by electing its representative bodies in at least three to five municipalities. It is estimated that decentralisation pilot projects will be held in Aileu, Liquiçá and Ermera.

Millennium Development Goals Suco Program

The Government will continue the Millennium Development Goals Suco Program that began in 2011. The Program seeks to build houses in villages, within a process of community progress. The houses will include solar energy, water and sanitation. The benefit of this project is that local communities will work alongside their most vulnerable neighbours, thereby ensuring that everyone has adequate housing.

National Program for Suco Development

The National Program for Suco Development, which seeks to accelerate development in all Sucos across Timor-Leste, was a program started in order to realise the goals of the *Strategic Development Plan 2011-2030*. However, the Government will be thoroughly revising and assessing this program and, if merited, the program may be cancelled pending the final formation of municipalities.

The Government is currently waiting the municipalities reform to be completed.

The goal of this program was to help communities promote their own development through planning, building and managing their own infrastructure. This program provides grants to suco communities in order to accelerate their access to services and to create employment within suco communities. However, it is now necessary to ensure greater control and oversight over these physical projects, so as to ensure better rationalisation of resources and their financial sustainability.

Trade

The Government will continue drafting trade policies in order to promote the development of its activities, including the management and organisation of municipal markets, the creation of facilities and conditions, and the definition of programs for supporting the movement of goods inside the country and abroad.

In terms of trade regulation, the Government will be proposing measures for regulating trade activities by creating standardisation and metrology systems, ensuring the implementation of a system of relatively constant price indicators and proposing preventive measures for safeguarding imported commodities, so that they do not breach the national standards set by Government or international standards.

In order to expand the market, it becomes imperative to socialise characteristic products with added economic value. This includes using the press and the media, both in Timor-Leste and abroad. As such, the

Government must have a marketing strategy and support producers and small industries, so that products may be introduced in the domestic and international markets.

In a first stage we will be focussing on products derived from bamboo, in close collaboration with the Institute for Research, Development, Training and Promotion of Bamboo. The Government will also continue to invest in trade infrastructure, such as transit and storage warehouses and leisure facilities, particularly those that have the greater chance of generating internal interest, in view of the national culture and tradition. The training and business capacity building of economic agents will also continue to be a priority, namely in cooperation with the Institute for Supporting Business Development (IADE).

The National Logistics Centre will continue ensuring the logistical needs of the State in a decentralised manner, as well as rationalising State interventions within the scope of public supply and normalisation of the prices of staple goods. As such, the Government will continue promoting the warehouses built in Tíbar, Bebora, Maubisse and Maliana, as well as continue to develop feasibility studies for constructing other warehouses and peeling machines in Venilale (Viqueque, Lospalos and Baucau), Natarbora (Manatuto,

Same, Aileu and Ainaro) and Maliana (Suai, Maliana, Liquiçá and Ermera).

Industry

The Government will continue to encourage the private sector to provide development services, particularly in the agribusiness area which will be a large feature of rural private sector development. The Government will encourage agribusiness services in the following areas:

- ✓ Market research;
- ✓ Market matching, such as facilitating contract farming agreements;
- ✓ Developing marketing strategies;
- ✓ Business appraisal and planning;
- ✓ Policy and advocacy;
- ✓ Training and technical assistance;
- ✓ Technology and product development; and
- ✓ Financing mechanisms.

The Government will also assist the private sector in providing basic farm inputs, such as seeds, fertilisers and sprays to farmers, by promoting the emergence of private sector agricultural support services. Private sector provision of training for farmers will be encouraged, with a focus on increasing incomes through agribusiness. With limited coverage by public extension services, farmers will be encouraged to be better educated and be given access to short duration training courses.

The Government will continue to support strategic agriculture extension – or training – campaigns. Industry experts will be required to develop extension and training materials to promote specific technologies and techniques or to address specific constraints, such as diseases for specific crops. Extension officers from the public and private sectors, including NGOs, will be trained on the application of these technologies prior to mobilising extension campaigns. Campaigns will be performance driven, have a wide coverage and encourage the emergence of private sector extension providers.

The Government will develop and execute agricultural extension campaigns and strategies concerning the cultivation of coffee, vanilla bean, candlenut, coconut oil and bamboo. The Government will also continue developing an industrial policy, drafting the key guidelines that will serve as the basis for executing short and long term industrial activities.

The creation of industrial hubs seeks to concentrate industries of the same type. It is particularly important that these industries are adapted to the realities and potential of each region of the country. During the first stage, the focus will be on developing transformation industries such as:

- ✓ Transformation of agricultural food produce for the internal markets (coffee, tempe tahu and tapioca, etc);
- ✓ Production of construction materials in order to replace imported construction materials (bricks, blocs, ceramic / natural rocks, etc.);
- ✓ Small manufacturing industries for replacing some imported agricultural food products, such as salt, water and noodles.

Cooperatives

The Government will continue to support the formation of cooperatives to encourage private sector growth in rural areas with start-up funding and grants for training, capacity building and cooperative monitoring, as well as other types of support, including in terms of acquiring equipment.

Cooperatives are an ideal model for rural communities to undertake private sector activity in a variety of areas ranging from managing bamboo plantations, to chicken farming, fishing and weaving. Government support will focus on building human resources and institutional capacity, by establishing a Training and Capacity Building Centre for Cooperative Groups, carrying out monitoring and advisory actions for micro companies and cooperatives, and providing in-kind subsidies to eligible cooperatives.

Grants will be available for in-kind equipment or tools that can be used to improve product quality, expand markets, establish market centres and promote products, as well as to improve infrastructure such as rehabilitating buildings to operate as cooperative headquarters.

Governance Development

Good governance and a professional, capable and responsive public sector are essential for the delivery of government services. Our public sector will also be the primary driver of economic growth in the medium term and will lay the foundation for our Nation's progress through developing our human resources and managing our infrastructure program. The Government will continue structuring the public service to reflect the realities of the Timorese situation and to best drive the economy and employment growth.

Planning and Strategic Investment

Designing, coordinating and assessing strategic planning and investment policies are essential for implementing the *Strategic Development Plan*, enabling a better rationalisation of financial resources and the achievement of the economic and social development goals of the country. As such, in 2017 the Government will give increased focus to:

- ✓ Planning, design and monitoring of strategic government programs and projects that promote growth, poverty reduction and job creation;
- ✓ Ensuring broad based investment and job creation at national, municipal and administrative post levels;
- ✓ Overseeing and monitoring line ministries and following the implementation of key programs.

These tasks will include economic planning and policy development in order to design approaches and initiatives that will lead development, economic growth, employment creation and industrial diversification in Timor-Leste.

In this sense, the Government will conduct extensive surveys in order to acquire data that is essential for executing the *Strategic Development Plan*. These surveys will take place in the following locations:

- ✓ Town of Suai, so as to enable urban planning that can absorb the delivery of services to the activities of the Supply Base. The planning also concerns water supply to the city and water collecting for agricultural activities, whose production must be high and permanent, so as to enable the existence and continuity of small and medium agribusiness companies;

- Towns of Aileu, Liquiçá and Ermera, in compliance with the plan for starting the administrative decentralisation process. Current towns will receive proper urban planning and their populations will be appropriately relocated, so that those administrative centres are gradually modernised. Timor-Leste's population is mostly young and will require a future looking view concerning the development of the country.

In terms of Strategic Investment, the Government will develop contacts and carry out thorough research in order to determine the possibility of submitting investment plans for the Petroleum Fund.

In coordination with the relevant ministries and agencies, the Government will also:

- Study and review mining proposals and a bill on the establishment of a Mineral Fund.
- Study, review and propose the creation of a financial structure, involving the Timorese Government, foreign banks and private entities, so as to respond to the needs of the national private sector. Whenever possible, these responses will have a regional perspective.
- Review investment proposals with social and economic impact as a result of employment creation.

- ✓ Give the due attention to the tourist potential of the country so that, in an integrated manner, we may start to make use of this potential in coordination with the sector of agriculture and fisheries, in order to create an agricultural industry.

Within the scope of strategic planning and investment, it will also be a priority for the Government to control and improve the quality of works, procurement systems and implementation of small and large projects in the area of infrastructure, including physical projects under the PDID (Integrated District Development Planning) and the PNDS (National Suco Development Program). The Government will be conducting thorough reviews concerning these programs, since to date there has not been a proper rationalisation of costs and the outcomes have not been satisfactory. It is urgent to make a decision on actual measures to ensure greater sustainability and quality of such projects.

In regard to Strategic Planning and Investment, the Government will be continuing the following programs:

- ✓ The National Procurement Commission, for appreciating large projects, ensuring quality, cost-efficiency and a high level of transparency, professionalism and integrity in the main infrastructure projects;

- ✓ The National Development Agency, responsible for assessing the main proposals concerning infrastructure and for monitoring and reporting on the execution of physical projects;
- ✓ The Infrastructure Fund and the Human Capital Development Fund, admitting multiyear projects so as to ensure the continuity of major programs investing in infrastructure and of programs to build the skills of Timorese human resources in strategic sectors.

Macroeconomic stability

The Government will further develop and improve its medium term macroeconomic framework in order to help quantify the fiscal resource envelope from 2012 to 2017. In particular, a policy on the extent of withdrawal of funds from the Petroleum Fund will be developed. This will set limits to the investments needed to support the *Strategic Development Plan 2011-2030* and encourage job creation in the economy and at the same time ensure that other key indicators such as the value of the petroleum fund and inflation are kept at prudent levels.

The macroeconomic technical working group will continue to involve several agencies in order to guarantee that the views of a range of stakeholders are included in the development of the macroeconomic framework. The Government will also strengthen the debt management capability within the Ministry of Finance, so as to improve the macroeconomic framework, and ensure that any Government borrowing serves for productive purposes that will have a net benefit for the entire people of Timor-Leste.

Reforming the Tax System

As the economy continues to develop, the *Strategic Development Plan 2011-2030* foresees that the tax base will expand from customs and trade to cover income tax and capital gains as well. The Government is currently reforming the tax system in order to improve the country's tax balance, which should also result in greater domestic revenue collection by the State.

At the same time the Government understands the need to attract investment through a competitive tax regime and free economic zones to attract private business. Hence, increased domestic revenue will have to come from broadening the tax base, closing loop holes and strengthening the administration of tax collection.

The Government will consider a range of possible fiscal changes including the possibility of introducing a Value Added Tax but any decision will be taken following extensive consultation with the

Timorese citizens, business leaders and other stakeholders to make sure that any changes work for the benefit the Timorese citizens.

Increased revenues will also come from managing autonomous agencies on a commercial basis so that profits are available to fund government initiatives. Using the profits of these organisations to provide essential revenues to support the program of Government will also mean that the Government provides greater financial oversight of these organisations.

Improving the ability of the national budget to deliver services

The Government will continue linking the Annual Plans of State Agencies more explicitly to the budget and continue developing financial reporting and monitoring tools enabling the people to see exactly how their money is spent and enabling the Government to have a better control over its operational spending.

The Government will also ensure that line Ministries are able to provide better services to the people by strengthening corporate planning, the budget execution process and the execution of physical projects. This will be done through training, as well as by strengthening the ability of line Ministries to use Government financial management software.

The Government will continue using these systems to improve the efficiency of Government expenses by introducing period offers for whole of Government procurements for items such as cars and computers to ensure better value for money and a standardisation of quality.

The Government will continue to improve the quality, accuracy, timeliness and usefulness of Government financial information by making sure all Government agencies are using these systems effectively and also continuing the process of reform of financial management software.

Increasing direct transfers of funds to municipalities and sucos

The Government will continue working to enhance its information system infrastructure, particularly with line Ministries and agencies in the municipalities. This will allow both better information and decision making in the rural areas and greater and more efficient disbursement of funds directly to agencies at municipality and suco level.

The Government will also continue working with the banking sector and expand its Treasury functions to the municipalities to allow for more direct transfers of funds at municipality and suco level. This will get funds directly to the places where they are needed most and help support the effort to stimulate the provision of credit in the more remote parts of our country.

Strengthening accountability systems

The Government will continue strengthening the monitoring, evaluation and accountability systems, by strengthening the monitoring and evaluation capabilities within key central agencies such as the Office of the Prime Minister and the Ministry of Finance. Detailed analysis such as public expenditure reviews will be undertaken regularly on a sector basis. These reports will be made public and will compliment on-going initiatives such as the citizen's guide to the National Budget.

Internal audit will also be strengthened across Government, particularly in the Ministries with larger structures and budgets, to make sure government officials are following correct practices and managing public expenditure in a proper manner.

Producing accurate and timely financial information for all stakeholders

The Government will look to continue the drive to improve the quality, timeliness, accuracy and availability of statistical data for our people. We will continue the process to develop and encourage the use of technologies such as the Transparency Portals and we will compliment this with a greater use of other media in order to make sure the information reaches all of our people. The Government will be committed to updating the Transparency Portals on a regular basis, by way of the current electronic financial system (GRP – Government Resource Planning System), and to providing real time information where possible.

We will continue drafting more frequent studies on household revenues and expenses in order to improve our understanding of the economy and to provide information for other key analytical work such as poverty analysis. We will also continue the program of regular long term studies, such as the 2015 census, which will enable us to have reliable data and indicators on the current situation of the country. Eventually, much of the statistical work will be carried out by an independent authority for the collation and distribution of national statistics.

Good Governance in the Public Sector

The civil service continues to require a sustained long term reform program to improve its capability to undertake its functions. Reform is needed in areas such as management and leadership, systems and procedures, administration, accounting and finance, budget execution and procurement, knowledge and document management, and strategic planning and monitoring.

Good governance in the civil service is also of central importance. It ensures trust and public confidence in government and in our democratic institutions. Transparency and independent accountability are not obstacles to effective governing; rather, they ensure that we are governed well and that the interests of our people are served. Good governance also helps to prevent corruption. The key principles of good governance are transparency, responsibility and accountability, integrity and leadership.

These principles drive good performance by promoting risk management, accountability for results, mechanisms for citizens to make complaints that can help to identify and address problem areas, and the proper use of public money. Transparency is the best protection against unethical behaviour and is the best way to achieve an ethical civil service culture and promote personal accountability.

Significant governance initiatives that have already been implemented include the following landmark reforms:

- ✓ Establishment of the Civil Service Commission;
- ✓ Establishment of the Anti-Corruption Commission;

- ✓ Increased powers of the Office of the Inspector-General to enable it to act independently when inspecting and auditing government ministries and agencies; and
- ✓ Establishment of the Audit Chamber under the Higher Administrative, Tax and Audit Court.

These reforms continue to progress in order to build a culture of accountability, openness and less bureaucratisation in our civil service, as well as to create important civil institutions that are independent of executive government. The Government will continue to support these reforms. In particular, it will support the Anti-Corruption Commission being provided with all the resources and funds that it requires to undertake its important mandate.

While significant progress has already been made in terms of reforming good governance and the public sector, it is necessary to continue these reforms so as to create a public sector that is able to meet the challenges ahead.

The Government will embark on a reform program that focuses on:

- ✓ Providing certainty amongst all civil servants regarding their functions, job descriptions, duties and responsibilities;
- ✓ Increasing the education levels, skills, knowledge and capacity of public sector workers;

- ✓ Instituting improved performance management and merit-based promotions;
- ✓ Improving information technology to support service delivery;
- ✓ Ensuring adequate knowledge and document management;
- ✓ Improving knowledge of and adherence to civil service values including professionalism, responsiveness, impartiality and non-affiliation in the performance of public tasks and services; and
- ✓ Developing a public sector organisational structure that is best suited to deliver the best possible results.

The Civil Service Commission will continue to be tasked with the role of implementing a long-term program to ensure that our civil service:

- ✓ Adheres to its values and code of ethics;
- ✓ Makes employment decisions based on merit and equity;
- ✓ Is professional, honest, dedicated and cooperating in defending national interests;
- ✓ Is politically impartial; and
- ✓ Has a strong service delivery focus.

This will be the role of the Civil Service Commission, in addition to tasks related with discipline and misconduct and the implementation of a grievance system.

The accountability of civil servants will be further improved through regular evaluation of performance against work plans. These performance reviews will focus on the achievement of outcomes and results. The performance management framework will be developed and driven by the Civil Service Commission, working with ministries and civil servants.

The Government will continue developing and implementing an intensive civil service human resource development program that is linked to our goals in terms of strategic development and efficient and effective workforce. This will involve the delivery of systematic, targeted and job-relevant training and professional development approaches.

The Government will build on Timor-Leste's foundation of good governance through the following policies and measures.

Public information

The Government is determined to ensure better communication with Timorese citizens, particularly those residing in remote areas and who may lack information that is updated and useful to their own development.

The Government intends to establish partnerships where everyone has a more active, responsible and interested participation, through what is known as a social audit. Governance indicators will be reviewed with greater exemption and responsibility, so that everyone takes part in improving service delivery to the Timorese people.

The Government website will continue to be improved, so as to provide information online on Timor-Leste and on Government activities. We will also increase the services available to Timorese citizens and develop the "e-Government" initiative.

The Government will also continue promoting gender awareness programs and public debates in the media, particularly on community radios and on the TVTL.

Seeking to ensure better coordination in terms of social issues, the Government will be creating an electronic coordination mechanism between the Minister of State responsible for Coordinating Social Issues and the communities located in remote areas. This will start with a pilot activity that will take place in three municipalities. Several other Government agencies are preparing their websites so that there will be sector platforms enabling more proximity and interactivity with the national and international public by 2017.

E-government

During the last few years it has become increasingly important for Governments around the world to communicate with their citizens using the Internet. The Internet is also the first place where people outside of Timor-Leste go to find out information about our Nation.

The Government will therefore continue to make information about Timor-Leste and Government activities available on-line and to increase the services available to Timorese citizens on-line through an "e-government" initiative.

We will build on the current Government website to link all government Ministries and agencies on a digital platform providing an interface between citizens and the government.

An improved system will also expedite the delivery of government services, by enabling easy access to services that can be provided on-line, such as renewing driver licences, requesting business registrations, requesting grants, forms and information on visas and taxes, paying for electricity and other utilities, requesting building approvals, submitting complaints against the civil service and contacting the Government. The e-Government will enable users to have access to all services made available by the Government and to have an interactive experience with Government Ministries and agencies, thereby improving service delivery in the public sector.

In order to achieve this goal, the Government will be creating the e-Government and ICT Unit, which will encompass various Ministries and be supervised by the Office of the Prime Minister. This Unit includes the planning of services, guidelines and strategies, the consideration of the best practices, technological solutions and communication platforms, the training of human resources and the raising of public awareness regarding the advantages of e-Government.

In addition to being responsible for developing and regulating all rules within the Government information system, this Unit will also be the main coordinator responsible for developing general Government policies concerning Information and Communication Technology.

Whistle-blower protection legislation

Whistle-blowers are civil servants or other officials who bravely report to the authorities acts of corruption, fraud and illegality they witness in their workplaces. This could include gross misconduct, corruption, maladministration, fraud or significant dangers to public health or safety. In order to protect whistle blowers from reprisals and harassment, the Government will strengthen the existent legislation, namely by having new legislation approved by Parliament to strengthen the legal regime protecting whistle-blowers against pressures and civil and criminal responsibilities if they disclose matters of public interest. This legislation will also protect people denouncing situations of government misconduct.

Code of Conduct for Government members

We will continue working to improve the draft Code of Conduct for Government Members, which was released recently. This code will provide strict rules and duties in regard to issues such as conflicts of interest and commercial activities, as well as information on the staffing and costs of ministerial offices. The Code will require all gifts above a certain value to be registered on a State gifts register.

Law on freedom of access to Administration documents

Transparency and government openness imply that citizens have the right to access information about them held in Public Administration databases. While the State in Timor-Leste still needs to strengthen its information and file management processes and its networked computer storage systems, the medium term goal is to promote freedom of access to information.

The previous Government introduced the need for legislation to be created by Parliament in order to provide citizens with the right to access information on them held by the Government, namely within the scope of criminal proceedings. While the international best practice provides exceptions for information that impacts upon national security, commercial confidentiality, individual privacy and the confidentiality of Council of Ministers discussions, the legislation will provide the broad right by all Timorese citizens to access government documents that have impact upon them.

Peace and Stability

The people of Timor-Leste fought against foreign occupation for 24 years without external assistance and eventually restored their country's Independence. The impact of the struggle created unique challenges in terms of consolidating internal security after independence.

However, Timor-Leste managed to overcome its crises and setbacks and to assume leadership over its strategic sectors, such as internal security. With the departure from the country of the International Stabilization Force and the United Nations Mission in late 2012, we are now considered to be a country that has learned from its weaknesses, invested in reconciliation and achieved an atmosphere of social and political peace.

In addition to the relationships of diplomacy and friendship that we have been establishing with virtually every country in the world, we are increasingly taking part in international forums, so as to share our challenges and accomplishments. The Government will continue working to ensure that Timor-Leste has an active participation in global and regional international organizations, giving its contribution towards international peace and stability.

Peace and Stability are key factors for national development. To speak of development is also to speak of justice and law. We will not succeed in building a fair country if we cannot ensure that justice is a cornerstone of our society and is accessible to everyone. As such, we must improve the way in which our agencies operate, which requires improving the skills of their staff. In turn, this requires a thorough assessment of the sector of justice and the establishment of a new cooperation framework that responds to the needs of the country.

The Government has also been working on the Strategic Concept of National Defence and Security, which is currently being debated in Parliament. This Strategic Concept sets the general and specific strategies in the areas of national defence and security concerning every governance sector.

Defence

The Government will ensure the modernization and professionalization of the F-FDTL, so that they are able to defend our Nation, support our internal security and contribute to efforts seeking to tackle threats against regional and global peace and stability. The F-FDTL must also be prepared to collaborate in situations of crisis due to public calamities, natural disasters and serious disturbances of public order.

Over the next two and a half years we will continue developing the military as a conventional professional defence force under democratic control. We will restructure and reorganise the F-FDTL to make sure it has the human resources capabilities for a high level of operational readiness for a broad range of missions.

We will establish a Defence Human Resources Management System in order to develop our soldiers, with a focus on addressing the areas of leadership, motivation, performance, cohesion, and decision-making.

The Government will continue to assess, monitor and address transnational threats such as organised crime, drug trafficking, terrorism, environmental degradation, climate change and natural disasters, as they may jeopardize the lives of our people. The Government will valorise the issue of the sea within the national defence strategy and diagnose the threats and opportunities faced by Timor-Leste in what concerns the proper configuration of how the Maritime Authority is to operate.

The Government will continue strengthening the National Defence Institute so that it can carry out its tasks in full.

The Government vows to continue supporting veterans, so that they can retire with the dignity they deserve. The Government will continue enabling women to have an increasingly greater role in national defence. The Government will also continue building the capacity of the F-FDTL Engineering Corps to be able to have an active participation in national development. We will strive to deploy F-FDTL into United Nations peace keeping operations and we will enhance our Command, Control, Communications, Computers and Intelligence (C41) systems capability by 2017.

The Government will continue to be committed at regional and international level, strengthening our participation in regional and international exercises. We will also continue developing technical and military cooperation with the various strategic partners of Timor-

Leste, as well as to contribute to the country's foreign policy and to strengthening trust in the form of a defence diplomacy and a strategy for peace.

Security

Being one of the essential duties of the State, security is a vital requirement for the exercise of the fundamental rights and liberties of the citizens. Security is necessary for preserving the stability of society itself and the normal development of the economic activity. Without security there is no room for development.

As such, the Government makes it a priority to adopt concrete policies and measures that contribute to making Timor-Leste a safer country, strengthening the authority of the State and developing and consolidating the efficiency of the Security Forces and Services. Security is an area where continued investment results in exponential advantages and benefits in the medium and long term.

In view of this, the Government will continue implementing a broad strategic plan that responds to the multifaceted reality and that covers issues as important as the prevention of risks for social stability, fighting crime, controlling maritime boundaries and areas, ensuring civil protection and preventing road accidents.

The Government will continue implementing the Internal Security Strategic Plan 2030 in order to ensure optimal performance in what regards peace, security and stability.

By 2017 the Government will be completing the 1st stage (2011-2015) of this Plan, which concerns the Strengthening and Consolidation of Security Bases. This 1st stage has two separate cornerstones: the Reform and Development of Security Agencies and the consolidation of Public Order and Safety.

In addition to monitoring compliance with the goals set for the 1st stage, the Government will start implementing the 2nd stage (2016-2020) of the Internal Security Strategic Plan 2030, which concerns the Expansion and Development of Internal Security.

As such, over the next two and a half years we will continue to strive to perfect the effective operational capacity in terms of preventing and investigating crime, as well as consolidating public safety and border control. We will also continue to encourage the community policing model and we will maintain public stability and safety as key responsibilities of the National Police of Timor-Leste.

The Government will continue focussing on the qualification of human resources and on the professionalisation of Security Agencies, guiding recruitment and training so as to meet current and future needs.

We will implement a new Disciplinary Regulation and a Statute for the members of the National Police of Timor-Leste. The purpose of these legal instruments is to enable better human resource administration and management in this Institution.

We will also establish a National Operations Centre, focussing on road safety. Additionally, we will train human resources in order to meet the growing challenges that Timor-Leste faces in this area.

The Government will also complete its program in what regards legal framework and support to the professional needs of Civil Protection, namely fire-fighters, in view of expanding it to the Municipalities.

We will also strengthen the National Directorate for Prevention of Community Conflict in order to consolidate trust and law and order in our communities. This will include the participation of the communities in the Municipal Councils of Security and in civic education programs.

In short, the Government will continue developing and consolidating Security Agencies within a logic of cooperation and complementarity, seeking to obtain the best results through the simplification, clarification and coordinated use of modern and adjusted means and processes.

Justice

Over the next two and a half years the Government will continue to strengthen the justice sector in order to consolidate stability, peace and the rule of law.

We will continue promoting the creation of a normative framework that befits a modern and progressive country. After the initial effort to revert the structural deficit in its legal framework and in the creation of a justice system able to ensure compliance with the basic rights and freedoms, the Government now seeks to reform the sector of justice and to draft a thorough study concerning law reforms, legislative standardisation and harmonisation, and the assessment of the need for intervention by the Government or by Parliament.

At a time when the basic justice infrastructures and services have already been created, the Government will now prepare to bring the justice system closer to the citizens. This entails informing the citizens of their rights and of the means available to them in order to defend those rights. This socialization process shall give priority to socially underprivileged citizens who lack the economic or social conditions to make use of the justice system.

The Government will continue to strive to ensure recognition of the supremacy of the law and the Constitution, thus contributing to the construction of a society that is freer, fairer and more equal. Consequently the Government will continue committed to strengthening the independence of the Magistrates, the autonomy of the Public Prosecution and the full exercise of the legal professions. The Government will ensure effective legal responsibility for the legitimate interests of citizens, particularly the weakest elements of society. In order to do this, the Government will create conditions to enable them to exert their rights, freedoms and guarantees in full, as well as set the proper mechanisms for citizens to have access to law and to the courts.

The Government will also continue its main task of building the legal and normative framework, assuring its harmonization and the unity of the legal order, always in accordance with the specific and actual Timorese context. In terms of legislation, the Government will seek to use simple language in order to continue to promote dialogue with the civil society and to enable public consultation during law-making. The Government will focus on the capacity building and specialization of its technical staff, so as to reduce as much as possible the dependence from international advisors and to promote the gradual replacement of international advisors with national counterparts.

Also in this area, the Government will give particular attention to creating measures that make the legal system truly bilingual. This will entail the promotion of the legal translation of laws, so as to ensure full and equal use of both official languages. The Government will also develop legal Tetum. These measures are essential for enabling Timorese citizens to understand justice and to have access to it.

The Government will also focus on making justice services available in the municipalities. On one hand, this will entail justice institutions, throughout the deployment of additional magistrates, prosecutors and public defenders throughout the territory. On the other hand, the Government will seek to make available public notary and registry services and services to promote and socialize rights and laws. Additionally the Government will regulate and promote alternative means for solving litigations, such as mediation, refereeing or conciliation, particularly in matters concerning labour, family or land disputes.

The Government will strengthen the institutional role of the Public Defence Office, increasing its autonomy from the framework of the Ministry of Justice. This is a vital justice institution that seeks to enable the pursuance of a true public service dedicated to ensuring access to law, by providing full and free legal and extrajudicial assistance to all citizens who lack the means to pay justice fees. Attorneys will also be able to rely on Government support, as the system of justice needs a pool of attorneys that are duly qualified and strong in technical and deontological terms, so as to be able to provide legal representation to the citizens.

The Government will carry out campaigns to raise the legal awareness of the citizens, by way of socialization and public education actions. This will focus particularly on the Municipalities with lower rates of trust in the formal system of justice.

The Government is trying to conduct an action with the purpose of raising awareness in the basic and secondary schools of the country. This action will be titled "Justice goes to school" and will seek to teach young students about our country's Justice system.

The Government will continue promoting the creation of a youth justice system, by adopting an education model in which the application of measures is determined by the need to educate children in the law and to promote their wellbeing, thus contributing to peace and order in society.

The Government will ensure the proper mechanisms for achieving a humane prison system that is fair, safe and directed to social reinsertion, favouring measures other than imprisonment and giving particular attention to young adults.

Within this scope, the Government is drafting a project to ensure the practical application of Suspended Sentences and Parole, which are already foreseen in the penal procedural legislation. The Government is also drafting the General Regulation on Prison Facilities, which is essential for guaranteeing the proper application of the recently-approved Penal Execution Regime.

Concerning key infrastructures, the Suai Prison Facility is currently being built, while the start of the construction of the Youth Centre, located in Tibar, is merely awaiting for the final approval of its budget.

Lastly, the Government has already selected the site for the Mental Health Centre and for the Baucau Prison Facility. Presently we are waiting for the necessary procedures to be completed so that the construction of both facilities may start.

The Government will continue to promote legal security and criminal justice by providing technical and human capacity building in the areas of criminal investigation, legal medicine and other forensic sciences, by strengthening its investigation capability and techniques, strategies and planning, collection and analysis of evidence, and techniques to investigate more complex crimes, such as organized crime, corruption, and money laundering, as well as domestic and sexual crimes. Importantly, the Criminal Investigation Scientific Police will be created and will start to operate.

The Government will also continue to be interested in strengthening the democratic control, verification and transparency bases, by way of the institutional building of the Audit Chamber.

The Government will continue to give particular attention to the process to regularize land property, promoting the registration of private property tiles and ensuring efficient mechanisms to manage public and private assets under the responsibility of the State. We will continue promoting the approval of the Land Law, which is vital for ensuring peace, social and economic development and domestic and foreign investment. As such, we will continue committed to legislating on this area, since otherwise we might be unable to achieve key projects of development and employment creation.

Essentially, Timor-Leste faces three types of challenges in terms of reforming land tenure: agricultural land under customary practices; urban land requiring clear "zoning" and property rights; and government land that may be used for public or private investment, under investment projects that, due to their size, nature or respective economic, social, environmental or technological impact, may have great interest for the country in accordance with the National Development Plan.

Here we should highlight the efforts being made in order to implement a modern system of systematic cadastral surveying, establishing reference points that enable the creation of a national geodesic network. We will also be standardizing geographic names and classifying soil usages correctly.

Acknowledging that the management of the real estate of the State is a vital issue within the development process, we are currently implementing a single information system for land registry purposes, for regulating and recording ownership and for taxing real estate.

The Government will be implementing fair and equitable rules protecting land ownership and transference. These rules must be in accordance with the interests of traditional owners and provide certainty and safety in relation to investments.

The system of justice is a pillar of the Rule of Law and one of the key sovereignty functions of the State. As such, the Government, through the Ministry of Justice, will continue to contribute to the qualification and sustainable development of the Rule of Law, to the reaffirmation of the universal value of fundamental rights, to the strengthening of citizenship and to the promotion of a society that is based on democratic, ethical and justice principles and values.

Foreign Policy

Timor-Leste has highly strategic geographic location and our natural resources wealth and our security will depend on maintaining good relationships with our neighbours and friends.

Our foreign policy seeks to protect and to promote the vital interests of the Timorese people, thereby safeguarding the independence, sovereignty and territorial integrity of our Nation.

Over the last few decades, countries generally experienced accelerated political, social and economic evolution, with different dynamics. The troubling scenarios we are witnessing in the various continents (Africa, Middle East, Europe, Asia and the Americas) tell us that Timor-Leste must draft and carry out a foreign policy that is adequate to the global circumstances. Matters like terrorism, extremism, ultra-nationalism, religious fanaticism, territorial disputes, economic and financial recessions and the unbridled race for natural resources may change and jeopardize the international order.

In this age of economic and technological globalization, no country, regardless of how far it is from the epicentre of events or the decision-making centres, is shielded from the impacts that may result from those epicentres and centres. The complexity of country relations requires the clear identification of priorities and challenges. We must anticipate changes and political, social and economic dynamics in the countries with which we cooperate, so that we can align our resources efficiently, adjust our perspectives, policies and acts and safeguard our national interests, without neglecting our role and our responsibilities within the international arena.

The Sixth Government will continue to develop special relationships with our neighbours, such as Indonesia and Australia, as well as with our development partners and friends throughout the world.

We will also continue to strengthen bilateral relations with our regional partners and to strive to join the Association of Southeast Asian Nations (ASEAN) and to strengthen the role of Timor-Leste in regional and international organizations such as the Pacific Islands Forum, the ASEAN Regional Forum, the Southwest Pacific Dialogue (SWPD) and the African, Caribbean and Pacific Group of States.

Timor-Leste believes that multiculturalism is an effective mechanism for solving global problems. As such, we will continue to take active part in multilateral forums, particularly in the General Assembly of the United Nations, as well as in international institutions and organizations that have relevance in the protection of our interests and of the universal principles in terms of peoples and states living together, such as human rights and democracy, environment, the fight against international terrorism, other transnational crimes and crimes against humanity.

Timor-Leste defends the fundamental principles of the Non-Aligned Movement and of the Charter of the United Nations concerning the preservation and promotion of world peace through dialogue and diplomacy between States, as well as preventing the use of force when solving conflicts.

Over the 2014-2016 biennium, Timor-Leste will be assuming the rotating presidency of the Community of Portuguese-Speaking Countries. The Sixth Government will continue with the efforts and initiatives seeking to meet the commitments made at the Tenth Conference of the Heads of State and Government and to strengthen cooperation and friendship between the members of this organization, focussing on economic and business cooperation.

We will also continue playing a proactive role in terms of international solidarity, based on international structures such as the g7+, a group dedicated to supporting fragile and/or conflict-affected nations.

In the area of Foreign Policy, one of our priorities is to ensure the delimitation of our maritime, land and air boundaries under the international law. The Council for Definitive Delimitation of Maritime Boundaries, approved by Parliament at the end of last year, will work so that Timor-Leste may effectively enforce its sovereignty powers within its national territory.

We will be leading an international cooperation approach, encouraging strong cultural, economic and commercial relations with other countries. This is vital for keeping active the conducts of innovation and investment that are essential to a young developing country. We will fine-tune our work methods and adopt the principles stated in the Paris Declaration, in the Accra Agenda for Action and in the commitments made in the high level forum in Busan concerning Partnerships for Effective Development Cooperation.

The Government will start drafting the general foreign policy guidelines of Timor-Leste, which will serve as a transitional instrument until the drafting of the White Book on Foreign Policy, to be completed by 2017.

Bilateral relations

In terms of bilateral relations, the Government will continue to follow our constitutional principle of having friendly relations with all countries in the world, regardless of their size, location or ideology.

We are located in a region of great political and economic dynamics, with competing geostrategic interests. Having good bilateral relations with our neighbouring countries is an imperative, rather than a choice. The ties and the historical trajectory of our country have enriched our identity as a nation and strengthened our relations with countries and peoples not only in our region, but also in other more distant continents.

We will carry out a thorough review of the situation and distribution of our diplomatic and consular representations, so as to make the necessary readjustments in order to respond to the new realities.

We will continue our excellent relationship with our closest neighbours Australia and Indonesia, while continuing to promote the historic ties of friendship with Portugal and with each of the CPLP countries.

We will maintain a strong a positive relation with the United States of America, in view of their valuable contribution to democracy, security, stability and development.

We will also continue cooperating with China, Japan and the Republic of Korea, which are economic powerhouses in the region of Asia.

We will strive to strengthen the ties of friendship and cooperation with each member of ASEAN and the European Union, with our friends in Africa and with Cuba and New Zealand, which have made important contributions in our path towards development.

As one of the two countries in the Southeast Asia with a greater percentage of Catholics, we will give particular attention to our relationship with the Holy See. We expect to sign the concordat with the Holy See by the end of the year, so as to further strengthen our ties with the Catholic Church.

Strengthening Institutions and International Relations

The Government will structurally readjust the Ministry of Foreign Affairs and Cooperation, in accordance with the Organic Law of the Sixth Constitutional Government of the DRTL, so as to promote the rationalization of its services and resources, to reduce bureaucracy and to nurture the general efficiency and effectiveness of the institution.

We will start rationalizing and resizing our diplomatic and consular representations, in accordance with the specific goals of each mission.

We will increment or reduce the number of representations abroad, as well as their resources, according to the needs.

We will conduct a thorough survey of the human, financial, patrimonial and material resources in existence in every DRTL representation abroad. We will also review the political framework and operation of these representations.

The Diplomatic Career Statute seeks to dignify the diplomatic office as a special career in Civil Service, as well as to list the set of rights and duties by diplomatic staff. As such, and until this Statute comes into force, we will be drafting a transitional diploma for regulating the key aspects concerning deployments, transfers, career progression and career promotions by staff members who currently hold diplomatic offices.

We will also be drafting a standalone diploma to regulate the transition of staff members who have performed or are performing diplomatic tasks in the Ministry of Foreign Affairs and Cooperation. This diploma will be approved alongside the Diplomatic Career Statute and will create an ad hoc Committee, as well as establish a list of criteria and ways of calculating career equivalence.

We will be investing in the greater professionalization and capacity building of human resources within the Ministry of Foreign Affairs and

Cooperation, so that they are efficient and able to perform different tasks, and that they possess the technical and diplomatic abilities for performing the duties given to them.

The Government will also be completing the curriculum for the Diplomatic Study Institute, which involves acquiring the necessary means for conducting training activities. The Government will then identify the training needs and draft an individual training plan in relation to every diplomat, so as to begin the systematized training of our diplomats in the Diplomatic Study Institute, in cooperation with other specialized agencies.

In order to ensure compliance, consistency and harmonization, the Government will be conducting a thorough survey of every international commitment binding the State of Timor-Leste, as well as listing every obligation by the State. The Government will then integrate these commitments and obligations within the national legal regime.

We will be giving priority to the Regulation concerning the Law on International Treaties, which thoroughly regulates the Law on International Treaties approved in 2010 and which targets the various stages of completion of international treaties signed by the State of Timor-Leste.

We will also carry out the proper harmonization of all national procedures and mechanisms concerning acts that bind the State or State agencies, so as to ensure that they are framed in accordance with the policy and priorities of Timor-Leste and that all responsibilities are met.

The Government will also focus on continuing the process for completing the Law on State Protocol Priorities, seeking to establish a standard for addressing senior entities and procedures to give dignity to entities.

www.ingramcontent.com/pod-product-compliance
Lightning Source LLC
Chambersburg PA
CBHW021105080526
44587CB00010B/393